ADVANCED TRAINING FOR THE DRESSAGE HORSE

ADVANCED TRAINING
FOR THE DRESSAGE HORSE

MEDIUM TO GRAND PRIX LEVEL

Tricia Gardiner

PHOTOGRAPHS BY BOB LANGRISH

WARD LOCK

A WARD LOCK BOOK
First published in the UK 1995 by
Ward Lock
Villiers House 41/47 Strand LONDON WC2N 5JE

A Cassell Imprint

Distributed in the United States by
Sterling Publishing Co., Inc.
387 Park Avenue South, New York, NY 10016–8810

Distributed in Australia by
Capricorn Link (Australia) Pty Ltd
2/13 Carrington Rod, Castle Hill NSW 2154

A British Library Cataloguing in Publication Data block for
this book may be obtained from the British Library

ISBN 0 7063 7147 X

Typeset by Litho Link Ltd, Welshpool, Powys, Wales
Printed and bound in Great Britain by The Bath Press, Avon

CONTENTS

Acknowledgements   6

1   The Early Training   7

2   The Advanced Way of Going   24

3   Lateral Work   45

4   Flying Changes   71

5   Pirouettes   92

6   Piaffe and Work in Hand   112

7   Passage   133

8   Freestyle to Music   147

Conclusion   154

Index   158

Acknowledgements

I would like to thank Domini Morgan, Bill Noble and David Hamer for their help with the text; my daughter Clare for the many long hours of typing; Carl Hester for working Alison Davis's horse Leonardo in long reins, and my friends Cynthia Llwellen Palmer, Caroline Shepherd, Claire Neilson and Tessa Thorne, who generously gave their time to work their horses for Bob Langrish to photograph.

CHAPTER 1

THE EARLY TRAINING

The early years of a dressage horse's career are spent establishing correct basic work. This basic work will remain paramount throughout the whole training right up to Grand Prix level, and particularly during the perfecting of this highest standard. There are two reasons why horses do not achieve success at this advanced level: the first is that they were not all born to be top athletes, and some find it physically quite difficult to perform a sequence of intricate and demanding movements in the correct balance and with the necessary collection; the second is that the initial basic training has not been sufficient to prepare the horse both physically and mentally for the ultimate goal ahead. If the muscles are not correctly developed and the horse's mind is not prepared by a systematic training programme, stiffness and tension will become part of the work – to the detriment of the end result.

The First Stages

The training of a dressage horse starts during his third to fourth year, depending on how mature he is. A horse that is born early in the year and is fed and kept in ideal conditions will be stronger than one born much later; a horse that has not had sufficient food or shelter from bad weather and has not been wormed at regular intervals during these formative years will be less physically mature. Young horses deprived of the care and attention necessary for good development may lag behind their more fortunate rivals until the age of five years, and this understandably affects their initial progress.

Before a horse is backed it is vital that he is strong enough to carry the weight of a light rider, and that the limbs are developed sufficiently to carry this extra weight without damage or stress. In the first stages of training, therefore, the muscles should gradually be strengthened, initially on the lunge and then whilst being ridden, so that the horse learns to move with the same impressive steps and natural body movement that he showed in freedom as a youngster – this ability makes him a good choice for training with the hope of producing a top competition horse. When the young horse is accustomed to the rider's weight, the basic training can commence.

There is an accepted list of requirements on which to establish the basic work. These can be thought of as the ABC of dressage training, and are as follows:

- Free forward movement, with each pace in the correct rhythm.
- Suppleness and co-ordination within the forward movement.
- Acceptance of the rider's contact and working on the bit.
- Submission and a willingness to work with the rider.
- Straightness.
- Impulsion, to develop the gaits and produce collection.

Until these objectives have been achieved to the extent that the rider is happy that the horse is progressing on the correct lines, it is pointless even to consider competing with him. Taking a young horse to a competition before the requirements of the Novice test can be executed with ease and confidence may cause him to associate entering an arena with unpleasant ideas and discomfort. This can then take some time to eradicate. For example, a horse that is stiff, not on the aids and too weak to carry a rider round a 20 × 40m arena easily can experience a painful and worrying five minutes being made to perform the movements, and in the future may not wish to co-operate when going down the centre line to halt at X. The basic training must be properly established first, and it can take up to a year before the horse is ready to compete in the Novice tests.

All aspects of a dressage horse's training are interrelated and any emphasis on one or another will depend on the particular horse and/or the difficulties he experiences. Problems, and improvements, can change during the daily work session depending on the horse's attitude to the work, and can be influenced greatly by the way in which the rider conducts the lesson and assesses the horse's temperament and physical ability, and his mood on the particular day. It is worth remembering that horses can also be very different to work after a couple of days off from their regular work pattern. Because of all these factors, the requirements are not listed in any special order.

Some horses are born with a naturally flawless rhythm and forward-going nature, moving in a supple and athletic manner from the start. Such horses do not require as much time spent on developing these aspects as a timid or nervous horse, whose movement and attitude to work may have been inhibited by the process of learning to carry a rider on his back and to be submissive. However, all horses must learn to accept the bit and obey the rider's aids, and only when this has been achieved can the horse be straightened and worked with impulsion. It is therefore important for anyone wishing to train a horse to Grand Prix level to appreciate the value of a systematic structure of training, which slowly builds and develops the horse physically and mentally into one that can perform at the very top. Refinement of the basic work will develop as the horse develops all the way through his training, and will act as a standby to fall back on if problems occur and the learning process has to revert to the simpler, more established work for a few days. This will help to restore confidence and relaxation, and satisfy the rider that there is a foundation on which to build.

Rhythm

At the end of each dressage test used in comepetition, a mark is given for the paces. The walk, trot and canter are assessed for the qualities of freedom and regularity, and the regularity of the natural steps taken in each gait is called the **rhythm**.

The **walk** has an even and purposeful four-time beat. If the interval between each step is not consistent or the steps are not of equal length, the rhythm of the walk is said to be 'impaired' or 'not correct'. Thoroughbred horses generally stride forward, showing good, correct walk steps. Warmblood horses do not naturally walk so well, even when unbroken and uninhibited in any way by a rider.

The walk is the most likely gait to be 'imperfect', because if the horse does not accept the contact, or for some reason becomes tense, the steps on the same side (right fore and right hind, or left fore and left hind) come to the ground almost together. This results in the walk deteriorating into a

A four-year-old (left) and a Grand Prix horse walking freely forward; both show pleasing, regular steps. The Advanced horse is more willing to take the rider's hand forward, with the nose in front of the vertical.

degree of pacing, and when viewed from the side appears to be a lateral or ambling movement. If the rider tries to collect and shorten the steps too early in the horse's training, these flaws in the purity of the pace can occur. In addition, if a one-sided contact is given to the horse an unevenness of the hind step will be obvious, because he will stiffen on the strong side and become tense and hold himself in the back.

Horses usually walk correctly when loose in the field and must be allowed to become accustomed to the rider's weight and walk in an unconstrained way during early training. Great care must then be taken when shortening the steps for collection. The rider should never resort to a strong contact on the reins nor use any force.

In **trot**, diagonal pairs of legs (off fore and near hind, and near fore and off hind) are lifted and put down to the ground in a two-time beat, with the forward-moving diagonal coming to the ground a moment after the lifting diagonal is raised, creating a moment of suspension. The trot loses

rhythm when either the diagonal steps are not of equal length, and therefore the front and back diagonal pair of legs are no longer parallel, or the spring and correct use of the joints is no longer evident and there is no real moment of suspension.

A good rhythm in trot cannot be maintained unless the horse is supple and in balance. Stiffness or loss of balance will cause irregularities to occur on turns and circles and during transitions. The rider can also cause unlevel steps by sitting more to one side of the saddle, by having one rein stronger than the other, and also by pushing the horse out of his natural stride by going too fast without the necessary impulsion and engagement.

The **canter** is an asymmetric three-time pace in which three separate beats are clearly heard in each stride. These beats are caused by one hind leg coming to the ground, followed by the other hind leg and diagonally opposite foreleg simultaneously, followed by the remaining foreleg.

This is the 'leading' foreleg. There is a moment of suspension, when all four legs are off the ground, after the leading foreleg comes off the ground and before the diagonally opposite hindleg starts the sequence of the stride again. Depending on which foreleg is leading, the horse is said to be going in 'canter right' or 'canter left'. If the forehand is making canter right and the hindquarters canter left, it is known as a 'disunited' canter. This is a serious fault, generally caused either by lack of co-ordination, lack of balance, or by the rider sitting awkwardly or not keeping the correct rein contact.

The rhythm of the canter is most usually affected by losing the moment of suspension. This in turn is most affected by the speed of the canter. For example, there is more likely to be an obvious lift from the ground in extended canter than there is during the pirouette canter, and in the canter pirouette itself there is no moment of suspension at all. In collection, when the suspension has been lost the canter looks very flat, and the beat becomes either hurried and tense or slow and laboured. This flatness occurs when the canter is slowed down without the hindquarters being actively engaged, or when the rein is kept too strong and does not allow the

A horse in canter with the off fore leading.

horse to use his head, neck and body in a natural way. Crookedness – when the quarters do not follow the path of the forehand – can be another cause of flatness.

With the help of modern technology, we can become more aware of the steps in canter by viewing them in slow motion on a video tape. It can then be seen that in fact the four-beat canter is very rare, and it is the moment of suspension that is missing when the canter appears untrue.

The **tempo** is the speed of the rhythm. It is important to develop the steps of each pace within the horse's natural rhythm. This can be first assessed on the lunge. Encourage the horse to settle down, relax and work at a speed that develops his own rhythm and at the same time teaches him to work in an outline that stretches his topline by relaxing the neck and back muscles. This will enable the horse to balance on a circle. As the horse relaxes, so the rhythm will develop, and if the horse is worked in this way he will muscle up correctly and become stronger. When the rider can work the horse forward in balance, encouraging him to use his body and joints in a supple and athletic way with increased engagement, the rhythm will be enhanced and look more spectacular – the paces are then said to have 'cadence'.

The same horse in a much shorter canter, showing the near hind on the ground following the moment of suspension.

Suppleness

Relaxation plays a big part in the modern training techniques of all athletic pursuits. If the muscles are not relaxed they are tense and stiff, a state in which they cannot work with maximum efficiency. The dressage horse has to learn to move in a supple, graceful way. This is then combined with impulsion and the maximum use of joints and muscles to develop his movement. When a horse looks supple he is also calm and confident, and his steps appear loose and unconstrained. He moves freely forward using his whole body, and when he learns to accept the rider's hand through the contact of the rein he is said to be 'working through'.

The work designed to develop the horse's rhythm will also result in a more co-ordinated, balanced and supple horse. The three requirements are interrelated, and one will not progress without the others. A mark is given at the end of each dressage test for the elasticity of the steps and suppleness of the back. If tension appears when the movements are being executed, there is a flaw in the basic training and the quality of the horse's work will not be up to standard.

The horse must be taught to carry the rider in a balanced way, so that he is in 'self-carriage'. It is the progressive ability to maintain balance during transitions and whilst performing turns, circles and lateral work that gradually enhances the suppleness and rhythm of the paces.

Contact and Accepting the Bit

Any horse will reject the feeling of the bit on the bars of the mouth or on the corners of the lips if the rider does not offer the horse a connection that is acceptable. It is up to the *rider* to improve this connection, particularly if the horse presses down on the hands because he has overbalanced or is disobedient and ignores the rein aids. It is difficult to describe the feel of a correct contact, but it should be one that gives confidence to the horse. A good contact feels elastic and springy, because the arms and shoulders are relaxed and can therefore maintain a constant and 'allowing' connection down the rein, with an even weight in both hands that stays with the horse as he moves his head and neck. The rider should allow the horse to take the hand forward when necessary because then, and only then, will the horse accept the bit. A horse will only accept a contact that is offered in a level and sympathetic way (see page 15 and 17).

OPPOSITE: *A perfect example of a balanced and active horse displaying suppleness and relaxation.*

A young horse showing a flexion to the left. The hind legs are directly in line with the shoulders.

When the horse accepts the contact he will have a relaxed lower jaw that does not set or cross under the top jaw. The lips should show a slight dampness or even quite a lot of white froth, signifying that the gullet is relaxed, which causes saliva to be secreted. The tongue should lie quietly under the bit and not draw back. The poll should be soft and flexible, and the horse willing to flex to either side. This flexion is a 'giving' of the jaw and a slight inclination of the head from the joint immediately behind the poll, so that the rider can see the eye of the side on which the flexion has been asked for, without a bend half-way down the neck. (For further information on bending, see Chapters 2 and 3.)

When a young horse learns to accept the bit and will take the hand forward and down with confidence, so that he stretches his top line into a truly rounded outline, he is then able to move forward with the most rhythmic steps he can produce in the early stages of his training, and is ready to be worked 'on the bit'. By this we mean that he is obedient to the aids and will make transitions without resistance. He can be ridden forward in all three paces without losing balance and gradually, as impulsion is created and he learns to step under from behind with his hindquarters becoming more engaged, he will stay in self-carriage and will not lean on the rider's hand, which would cause the quality of the rein contract to deteriorate. The ability to contain impulsion and work through the rein in a loose and unconstrained way can take a long time to achieve. The horse's neck should not be shortened or the nose made to come behind the vertical for any length of time. When the weight has been transferred to the hindquarters correctly, the poll should be the highest point of the body.

Submission

Initially, when the horse is backed he learns to accept all the necessary equipment, be obedient to the voice and respect the lunge whip. When first ridden, he must allow the rider to control him by responding to the aids that the rider gives with his weight, legs and hands. This basic submission is then refined as training progresses and the horse develops trust and confidence in the rider. Mentally, the horse must allow the rider to communicate, and accept willingly the work the rider has carefully planned to improve the horse's physique and develop the aspects already mentioned without causing tension, resistance or stiffness. An unsympathetic

A four-year-old horse working freely forward on the bit.

rider can bully a horse into being obedient, but this is not the classical method with which the rider will produce the best-quality work.

For true submission, the horse works willingly through the rein and responds to all requests asked of him. He understands the aids with confidence and appears to want to please his rider and work as a partner in trust and harmony, producing graceful movements without any apparent effort.

Impulsion

Chambers 20th Century Dictionary describes impulsion as 'an impelling force', and 'to impel' as 'to urge forward, to excite action'. In dressage we are looking for controlled impulsion, with the horse thinking forward and ready to move forward in an active and athletic way whenever the rider wishes. However, we must also be able to contain the impulsion and teach the horse to swing over his back and, with the increased bending of the joints, move with elasticity and suppleness.

As training progresses and the weight-bearing capacity of the horse's hindquarters increases, the hind legs will step further under the body, lowering the haunches and raising the forehand, giving the horse the appearance of moving slightly uphill. When this happens the rider has achieved 'collection'.

Creating impulsion and being able to contain it correctly is the most difficult element in producing an advanced dressage horse. If this part of the training is not approached with care and a great deal of feel on the part of the rider, the horse will not learn to take the shorter, more active steps made possible by increased mobility of all the joints. Instead, he may tighten in his neck and come up against the rider's hand, which could lead to him making unlevel steps and losing the quality of the contact. The spring and rhythm in the steps that has been developed in the novice horse must not be damaged by an unsympathetic or forceful rider trying to contain extra impulsion in an advanced way of going.

Straightness

Unless the hindquarters are directly in line with the shoulders, a horse cannot make full use of his haunches to propel himself forward or to bend all the joints and push upwards. When looking at the horse's footprints on an unmarked surface, the hind feet should follow the prints on the fore feet whether they are on a straight line or a curve. The horse's spine should appear to be on a similar line, which means that the neck should not bend more than the body unless the rider specifically positions it differently during training. Horses are rarely straight by nature. Just as humans are right- or left-handed, horses also find it easier to do things on one side. The stiff side of the horse is more difficult to soften and move sideways with a bend. The soft side is more difficult to straighten and control the shoulders.

Straightening the young horse happens gradually as the muscles develop and the other requirements become confirmed – a rider cannot get on an untrained horse and demand straightness. However, this aspect must be considered throughout the training and, having progressed from the early stages, it is something that will always need correcting, even when the horse has reached Grand Prix standard. In the more advanced tests there are many transitions on the centre line where the judges can see the slightest deviation of the

Working forward into the rein, looking attentive and submissive.

shoulders or hindquarters, for example, from rein back into passage, passage into piaffe, and into the halt or a strike off into canter. It can therefore be appreciated how important it is to develop the straightening process as early as possible.

One of the first signs that the young horse feels different on either side of his body is an unevenness in the rein contact. On the stiff side there will be heavier pressure, because the horse is not in self-carriage and relies on the support of the rein to help balance himself. If the weight is on the forehand, the shoulder on the stiff side will fall out as it takes more weight, with the result that the hind-quarters do not follow. The horse is then said to be crooked.

A horse moving with impulsion in extended trot.

This horse is in position left, whereby the rider can control any tendency of the shoulder to fall to the right and therefore keep the horse straight.

Encouraging the horse to take more contact on the lighter rein will in itself help to straighten the body. Circling, bending and gradually stretching the muscles on the soft side, and relaxing the muscles on the stiff side, will enable the rider to release the stronger contact and so even up the pressure down the rein. Eventually the rider should achieve a similar feel down the rein in each hand.

The most important exercise for straightening the horse is shoulder-in. This cannot be done until the horse is moving forward well, accepting the hand and staying in a round outline when the rider uses the basic leg aids. However, when the time is right and the shoulder-in can be used to gain control over the shoulders and engage the hindquarters in walk, trot and canter, the straightening process will not be difficult (see Chapter 3).

Competing at Novice and Elementary Level

A horse and rider are ready to start competing at Novice level when a satisfactory degree of the requirements discussed above has been achieved. The tests are designed to show the simple movements of circles, turns and progressive transitions that should have been incorporated by degrees into the daily work routine as a matter of course. It is only the requirement to make these transitions by the correct marker, and to proceed in the desired gait with the correct outline for a set duration of time, that makes the test a little more difficult than the normal work pattern.

The rider should be aiming to show the judge that the horse goes freely forward, maintaining regular, correct footfalls in all three paces and showing the relaxed athleticism which is the hallmark of good working paces. When asked for lengthened strides in trot and canter, the horse should not hurry. Energetic flexion of the hocks will allow the hind feet to come to the ground well under the body of the horse, carrying weight as well as pushing forward with a swinging back.

The horse should be in self-carriage and not relying on the bit for support. He should happily accept a light, consistent contact, with the poll as the highest point and the nose not coming behind the vertical. The outline should be natural and not forced, the result of willing, balanced obedience, working forward from the rider's legs into sympathetic and allowing hands. There should be no resistance, particularly in transitions. The hind feet should follow the track of the front feet, so that the horse remains straight on all straight lines, and correctly bent in corners and on circles.

The rider should assist the horse's balance by sitting straight, without stiffness or more weight on one side of the horse's back than the other. The rider's lower legs should be softly close to the horse's sides and his arms held without stiffness, so that the aids may be both effectivce and imperceptible.

It is not obligatory to ride in sitting trot at Novice level, so I would advise riding in rising trot until such time as the horse is properly relaxed and working over his back. Only then will he not feel hard and tense to sit on.

Elementary level follows on progressively from the Novice. The horse should look stronger, because his muscles have been developed by working him in a more supple and active way. As well as the movements in the Novice tests, the horse must be able to make shoulder-in, counter canter, simple changes and rein back. While performing this more difficult work the paces must remain regular and with the correct footfall. When he is asked for the medium paces, the horse should lengthen his stride freely without hurrying, showing lightness and rhythm.

The Elementary horse will carry a little more weight on his hind legs than the Novice horse, and this will enable him to become lighter in the forehand and show elasticity of steps, in turn enabling him to shorten and lengthen his stride as requested without any loss of balance. A consistent, light contact with the bit should be happily maintained throughout, particularly in transitions, both within each pace and from one pace to another. The improved balance will then make it easier for the horse to develop his paces and lengthen his outline when he lengthens his stride, and to shorten his outline as he works towards correct collection, with the strides becoming shorter and a little raised due to the increased engagement of the hind legs.

When asked to show shoulder-in, the horse should be bent around the rider's inside leg, maintaining his balance, impulsion and regularity without resistance. The rider must be careful to prevent the hindquarters swinging out.

The rider should have a supple seat and be able to absorb the increased movement over the back of his horse, so that he can engage the hindquarters to a greater extent than at Novice level. He will ensure that the horse is in balance before each movement or transition, and position the horse so that it is straight on all straight lines and correctly bent in corners and on circles. At this level the rider has to sit for all the trot work.

The Novice, Elementary and Medium level tests do not present a great deal of difficulty to the well-balanced, athletic and correctly trained horse, particularly when he is presented by an experienced and dedicated dressage rider. It is even possible to reach Medium level on a horse that has sensational movement and physique but has not necessarily been through the correct training. Such a horse can appear to be round in his outline without actually accepting the rider's hand in the true sense, and therefore will not be working through correctly or stretching his neck and back when asked. His movement can be naturally so rhythmic and springy that he can steal marks at the lower levels without being 'in front of the rider's leg'. However, if this has been the case the shortcomings will show up at Medium level, where a greater degree of control of the shoulders must be evident, especially in the lateral work, the execution of the more difficult movements and transitions, and the beginnings of collection.

The young horse that upgrades very quickly may need some time out of competition whilst the more advanced way of going is being consolidated. This is particularly true while he is learning the flying changes. If the rider has a very talented horse, the competition strategy will need to be considered carefully. There are two main options: compete with the young horse, which may upgrade very quickly and then need some time away from competition while the advanced work is being established; or train the horse to a fairly high standard at home before serious competing begins. I favour the latter approach, as it ensures that the horse is not over-exposed initially and therefore does not develop unwanted attitudes or bad habits in the arena due to insufficient training, which a clever rider may be able to disguise. This may later become a nuisance, and detrimental to the horse's correct way of going and further training. The rider should not get into the habit of covering up training problems at home as he or she would in a test. When training at home the problems must be felt and then corrected constructively as they occur.

It is not advisable to compete excessively on a young horse in the 20 × 40m arena, particularly on hard ground, which is often the case in the summer, and deep mud in spring and autumn. The more advanced tests are usually held on an all-weather surface or in an indoor school, which saves the gaits being inhibited by unyielding going. The 20 × 60m arena is far easier for a big-moving horse to work in, and the less he is asked to compete in the smaller arena the better.

In short, the saying 'take time but don't waste time' could not be more apt when considering the correct basic training of a young dressage horse. The rider should take time to establish the essential basic requirements and ensure that the horse understands and responds to clear and precise aids, so that he can work forwards in balance and with confidence. However, the rider should also recognize by 'feel' when more demands can be placed on the horse to establish the solid foundation on which the advanced work can be built.

CHAPTER 2

THE ADVANCED WAY OF GOING

Medium and Advanced Medium

When the horse has reached Medium level the first step on the advanced ladder has been attained. This can take two to three years from the start of the horse's training, depending on the rate at which he develops during that time.

The requirements for a Medium horse are that all three paces should be correct and regular, and should also show lightness, cadence and freedom. At this level the horse is for the first time required to show truly extended paces. This means that when the horse is extending, the angle of the hind cannon bone and that of the extended front leg should be the same, demonstrating that the extension is coming correctly from behind. The toe of the front foot – never the heel – should point towards the ground at the moment of greatest extension.

The increased engagement of the horse's hind legs will result in lightening of the forehand and freedom of the shoulder. This will allow the Medium horse to develop the elasticity and cadence of his trot and canter, with clear definition between the collected, medium and extended work. The increased suppleness of the back enables him to fulfil happily all the requirements of the Medium tests, without any stiffness or resistance.

The whole outline of the horse should now be rounder, with the head carriage higher and the poll always the highest point. For the outline to be correct, the nose must not come behind the vertical. This improved balance will have developed because the back is now rounder and more weight is being carried by the hind legs. In all lateral work, the bend around the rider's inside leg and the correct angle should be

OPPOSITE: *A horse in extended trot, showing how the heel can come to the ground first if the foreleg is thrust forward without the neck lengthening.*

maintained without resistance or any loss of impulsion, balance or regularity of the paces. All transitions must be clearly defined and there should be no loss of rhythm, straightness or elasticity.

The rider must have developed an independent, supple seat which enables him to 'go with' the horse's movements and allow the horse's back to swing without the rider losing his position. His aids should be effective and yet almost imperceptible, demonstrating a harmonious partnership with his horse.

A little more is expected from the Advanced Medium horse. The quality of the paces should now be more impressive. In the extended paces the horse's frame should lengthen clearly and all transitions should be well defined, both from one pace to another and within each pace. There must be no loss of rhythm or straightness. The collected movements should show increased activity and suppleness of the hindquarters and lightness of the forehand. The horse should accept the bit confidently with a light, consistent contact and with the poll as the highest point.

Half-passes in trot and canter should flow easily on two tracks, with the impulsion, rhythm and correct angle being maintained throughout. At this standard single flying changes are required for the first time. The quality of the canter should be sufficiently light and active for the horse easily to show calm, straight yet expressive flying changes. Approximately six single flying changes are made during the canter part of the tests; otherwise, the movements at Medium and Advanced Medium level are very similar:

● Entry in collected trot or canter.

● Half-pirouettes in collected walk.

● Rein back followed by a transition into canter.

● 8m and 10m circles and half-circles in collected trot, along with shoulder-in, travers and half-passes at an easy forward angle.

● 8m and 10m circles and half-circles in a collected canter, canter half-pass, counter canter and simple changes.

Along with the usual transitions, separate marks are also given for the transitions from extended or medium paces into collected paces and vice versa.

The desire to go happily and freely forward should

contribute to the impression that the horse is performing the movements of his own accord in harmony with his rider. The ease with which both horse and rider fulfil the requirements of the tests at this level should demonstrate that they have achieved a sound basis from which to progress to the more advanced Fédération Equestre International (FEI) tests.

LEFT: *A Medium horse in shoulder-in left.*

RIGHT: *A Medium horse in half-pass left.*

Advanced

At this level the rider must show that the horse is capable of correct collected, medium and extended paces in all three gaits. The more advanced way of going already described must improve steadily at each level up to Grand Prix. The half-pass, pirouettes, flying changes, piaffe and passage, along with the ensuing transitions, will increase in difficulty. There is no value in performing a movement without the required suppleness, balance and impulsion necessary to show that the horse has been correctly trained up to Advanced standard.

Prix St George

Prix St George is the easiest of the FEI Advanced tests used at official international competitions. At this standard the entry is always made in collected canter and the transition into and out of halt must not be progressive. The movements are:

- Half-pirouettes in collected walk.

- 8m circles, shoulder-in and half-pass in collected trot, including a simple counter change of hand.

- Similar half-passes in collected canter, along with counter canter, half-pirouettes, single flying changes and a sequence of four-time and three-time flying changes.

When giving marks the judge is required to place even more emphasis on the transitions than at the previous levels.

Intermediare I

At this level the horse must show established half-pirouettes in collected walk. There is also a movement that requires the horse to rein back, walk forward and rein back again for a set number of steps without halting in between (in Germany this is known as the *Schaukel*). This movement shows the judge that the horse is truly submissive and obedient to the rider's aids.

The canter work at this level is more demanding, including such movements as the canter serpentine with the particularly difficult counter canter, and a counter change of hand down the centre line of four steps to the left, eight to the right, eight back to the left and then four to the right again. The horse must also show canter pirouettes, a single flying change from medium canter, and sequences of flying changes every three and two strides. These movements will test whether or not the horse has developed a greater degree of collection and the basic training has been correct.

Intermediare II

This includes a similar pattern of rein back to the Intermediare I. However, the trot half-passes are at a steeper angle, which requires more suppleness and agility, in its turn developed from a higher degree of collection and impulsion. This level also includes seven to eight steps of piaffe, with a forward progress of 1m (1yd) being permitted. The horse is also required to show passage for a short distance, and the transitions incorporating piaffe and passage are marked for

OPPOSITE: *A Grand Prix horse in passage, in a round outline with no tension or resistance.*

28

the first time. Canter pirouettes are now of 360 degrees, and there is a similar counter change of hand in canter to that required in the Intermediare I. The horse must show a sequence of nine two-time and nine one-time flying changes.

Grand Prix

At this level the horse must show work that is near perfection. The piaffe must be of 12 to 15 steps and for high marks should be performed on the spot. The passage is of much longer duration and there are many mark-earning transitions involving piaffe and passage. In canter there are five counter changes of hand in half-pass down the centre line, with flying changes at each change of direction. The first and last half-pass are of three strides and the other four of six strides. This is an extremely difficult movement for both horse and rider, requiring great concentration and feel on the part of the rider to give the horse the correct aids at the right moment, repositioning him every six strides in order to perform the half-pass without error. In addition, 360-degree canter pirouettes to both right and left are ridden on the centre line, requiring great control, and 15 one-time flying changes are ridden across the diagonal.

A Novice horse (left) and a Grand Prix horse in working trot. The difference in self-carriage and development of the muscles is clearly visible.

Grand Prix Special

This test is the most difficult, and the highest goal for a dressage horse and rider – the winner of this test at an Olympic Games will receive the gold medal. It includes all the movements of the Grand Prix test, but they are arranged in a more difficult pattern, and include transitions from extended trot into passage and vice versa, and nine one-time flying changes between the canter pirouettes on the centre line. The horse that is capable of performing these movements without tension or resistance demonstrates that he has followed a training programme that has enhanced and developed his physique, agility and suppleness.

Teaching the Advanced Movements

It is vitally important during dressage training to progress up the ladder one step at a time. If the trainer is in a hurry and takes short cuts by missing out every other rung there will be penalties to pay – the end result may not be as perfect as desired, and this will become increasingly apparent. The training must be constructed in a logical way in order to give the horse every chance of achieving the goals set for him.

Development of Balance and Musculature

The development of the horse's muscles will show clearly whether or not the earlier work has been executed correctly. With correct development, his neck and back will be strong over the topline, and his hindquarters will look as well proportioned as the forehand. If the muscles on the haunches look weak and the spine stands up from the back due to lack of the musculature on either side of the spine that would indicated strength and power, or the muscles on the chest and forearms are harder to the touch than those of the gaskin and thigh muscles on the inside of the hind limbs, the horse has not yet transferred enough of the carrying power to his hindquarters. This means that he is not yet in an advanced balance and light in the forehand, and in this situation he may well at times seek the rider's hand for support, and if viewed from the ground will appear to have his hind legs trailing rather than stepping under his body.

If a horse is introduced to the advanced movements when he is not yet in an advanced way of going, many of these movements will present unnecessary difficulties and he will stiffen against them, as he is not yet physically able to do what is required. He may even develop a grudge against performing what is asked, which will result in resistance and irregular paces.

In fact, some movements are far more demanding than others. For instance, a horse that is still a little on the forehand can learn flying changes quite easily and, if he has a good temperament, can progress to tempi changes without much problem. However, if he is not well balanced he will come 'croup high' as he makes the flying change (see Chapter 4) and even use the flying change steps as a means of pushing his shoulders down, therefore moving his weight from his haunches on to his shoulders. If this is done in the tempi changes, at the end of the diagonal line the horse will no longer be collected and, even if the changes have been without fault, will loose a mark because of this.

A very demanding movement for the young horse is the canter pirouette. Unlike the flying change, this cannot be made without self-carriage. The horse has to be able to canter at walk speed for a few steps and put weight on the haunches, while the shoulder is moved round 180 or 360 degrees. If the horse is forced to do this movement when he is tense, stiff and unbalanced he will find it very uncomfortable, set himself against the aids and lack the relaxation and suppleness to use his joints and lower his haunches in the correct way.

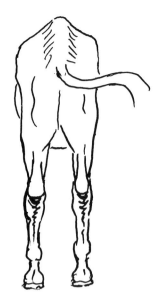

Poorly muscled hindquarters.

A weak neck lacking correct musculature.

Once a horse has started to associate a movement with discomfort, it is very difficult and time consuming to eradicate that feeling from his mind, and therefore time is well spent working the horse up to the correct way of going in walk, trot and canter before teaching advanced movements and possibly running into trouble because he is not yet ready for them. Always make it easy for the horse to do things, and analyse the movement being taught in great detail, as is the normal procedure in other athletic sports. It is very important to check that the horse understands every small part before putting it all together.

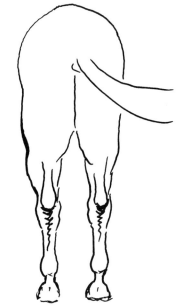

Powerful, well-muscled hindquarters.

A well-muscled horse showing a correctly developed topline.

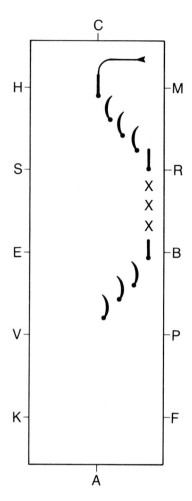

Half-pass to walk from canter left. Walk a few steps to get the new direction and strike off into canter half-pass right.

Teaching Advanced Movements: An Example

The following is an example of teaching the horse an advanced movement in a progressive and logical way. When the horse has learned to canter half-pass for Medium and Advanced Medium tests, the next step is to make a counter change of hand. This is where the half-pass to the left is followed by a flying change of leg, and the horse then moves off immediately in half-pass to the right. This can be started by making a few steps of canter half-pass to the left; then come back to walk as in a simple change and, before making the strike off into canter right, position the horse in shoulder-in right and then ride half-pass to the right. When the horse is accustomed to doing this, a flying change can be substituted for the simple change, but the horse must not be asked to make the half-pass in the new direction until he is in the correct position. This may entail some steps of canter on a straight line before adopting the different bend around the rider's new inside leg.

In this way the movement is broken down and taught to the horse so that he understands what is wanted. He will then not become tense and throw his weight on to the new inside shoulder, which would result in a half-pass without the correct bend.

Loosening Up

It is not possible to obtain true collection without suppleness and the advanced horse must be given sufficient time at each training session to loosen up. I favour a routine whereby the horse is worked and then turned out each day for a few hours. This freedom and period of relaxation will help to keep his mental attitude tranquil, as well as being beneficial to the muscles, as the horse is given a chance to move about in a relaxed way rather than being confined in a stable for almost 24 hours.

If the horse cannot be turned out he should either be walked in hand or on a loose rein when being ridden, thus starting the loosening-up process slowly. Many horses benefit from being lunged before the rider starts work, letting them stretch the topline and loosen the back muscles without the rider's weight.

Lungeing has many advantages, especially if the horse is upset by new surroundings or the competition atmosphere, or if he has spent many hours travelling in a horsebox. The rider will soon discover the most beneficial way to prepare

A horse being walked on a loose rein to loosen up.

each particular horse for the daily work session or for riding-in for a competition. Every horse is different and must be treated as an individual.

However, I believe they should all start work by stretching the neck down, as by doing so they will free the neck and back muscles. This position should be started in trot, without very much impulsion at first. Then, as the contact on the rein is accepted and taken 'forward and down' with the the rhythm established, the horse must work energetically

A horse working well forward and bending around the rider's inside leg.

through from behind, taking big, active steps and gradually using his body in the correct way. The rider should feel the back coming up under the saddle, and if you watch the horse from the ground the muscles behind the saddle should be seen rippling and swinging with each step. Cantering in the same position will also help to loosen up the back, as will canter-trot-canter transitions and making sure that the neck can be bent to each side.

It is much easier for the horse to bend his neck when it is long and stretched down than when it is higher and short, and bending the neck in the lower position willl loosen muscles that can become very tight. However, to be correct it should be possible to release the inside rein with the horse remaining around the rider's inside leg and maintaining the curve. The outside rein should be accepted and taken forward, as one would expect when the more advanced exercises are used.

Bending and Different Outlines when Working the Horse Down

Bending the horse is discussed in some detail in Chapter 3, particularly in relation to lateral work. However, before lateral work has been established the horse should be willing to let the rider position the neck to either side of the shoulders, especially when the horse has taken the rider's hand forward and down to stretch the topline. This helps to break down any resistance in the neck and makes the horse more mobile in front of the saddle.

The horse cannot bend around the rider's inside leg until such time as he is relaxed, supple and has the mobility to obey the riders' wishes to this end. I like to establish that the horse is 'bendable' long before starting to ride in collection, and often ask the horse to yield to the inside leg and bend him in the neck whilst pushing him to the outside of the bend. This exercise, made in either direction in a forward working trot, will loosen the shoulder. If performed on a large circle it will also help to engage the inside hind leg.

The rider must be careful to flex the horse at the poll and not bend the neck half-way down, as when this happens there is a danger of losing control of the outside shoulder. The horse should be flexed to the inside by turning the head very slightly at a point just behind the poll, or curving the neck symmetrically from the withers to the poll at an angle controlled by the rider. When this position is reinforced by the rider positioning and controlling the horse's body around his inside leg, the horse is in shoulder-in.

The horse must learn to bend over his topline as well as laterally, so the initial stretching down to loosen him up must be developed with this in mind. As the horse loosens up he must be ridden well forward to engage the hind legs, and worked on circles to encourage him to bring his back up under the rider. When this way of going is correct, it can be likened to a horse stretching his topline and rounding correctly over a fence.

It is important that the rider appreciates the difference between:

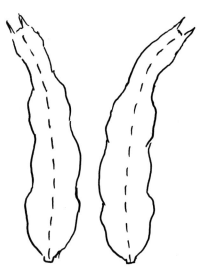

More bend in the neck than in the body (right). The horse's spine following the line of a curve (left).

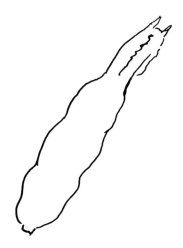

A flexion to the right.

37

● A horse that is being worked in a deep outline, but because he is working through from behind and using his back, stays up in the shoulder and uses his body correctly as he seeks the rider's contact. This is the correct way to work a horse 'down' or 'deep', with the object being to stretch and supple the topline. (See 1 opposite.)

● A horse that lowers the head and neck but drops the bit and comes behind the vertical, and is therefore not working into the rider's hand with activity coming through from behind. (See 2 opposite.)

● A horse that is allowed to take the hand down, but then leans on the bit without any self-carriage or engagement. This horse will be down on to his shoulders and therefore on the forehand. (See 3 opposite.)

Horses rounding over a fence.

Having the Horse Between the Inside Leg and Outside Rein

The process of being able to give away the inside rein when the horse is in a curved position around the rider's inside leg, so that the horse remains in that position until asked to straighten, is one way of demonstrating that the horse is 'between the inside leg and outside rein'. Basically, this is a situation that signifies that the rider has more control, and that the training is developing along the right lines. If the horse is accepting the outside rein correctly and taking the contact forward, he should stay on the line of a large or small circle when the inside rein is given away or, a more difficult situation, stay straight up the centre line, having turned on to it correctly bent around the inside leg. The same applies to shoulder-in. If the inside rein can be released and the horse stays in the correct angle and bend on the desired line, he is properly between the inside leg and outside rein.

It is also important to check that the horse is accepting the inside rein properly. This can be done by giving away the outside rein, and if correct, the inside of the neck should not develop any more bend, nor should the rein get stronger or the head tip. In addition, the horse should not increase his speed.

The giving away of either or both reins simultaneously is a

These photographs show the difference in outline between the Novice (left) and Advanced horse.

means of checking the balance, control and acceptance of the contact. With this in mind, this exercise should be done at intervals during the training session in walk, trot and canter.

Having the Horse in Front of the Leg

Another important feeling to have when training the advanced horse is that of keeping the horse in front of the rider's leg. This feeling alters slightly as the horse becomes more balanced and collected.

The novice horse that is in front of the leg will move freely forward in any gait when asked, learning to use himself from behind without falling on to his forehand. This is aided by the rider, who monitors the speed and makes the necessary transitions and half-halts.

As the training progresses and collection starts to develop, the influence of the leg will take on a new directive. The rider must always feel that he is riding forward, but the horse must be taught to increase impulsion without always increasing the speed. For example, if, when riding a half-pass, the rider feels that the steps are not active enough, he should be able to use the inside leg to increase the impulsion as the horse moves sideways, so that the steps appear more active and the horse moves with increased spring, but does not necessarily

An Advanced horse showing a collected trot, with the energy contained and coming up from the rider's leg.

go faster. If the rider can create this impulsion whilst riding movements, and use his legs effectively but still keep the horse light in the rein, he will be able to ride forward to show extended paces when required and yet still be able to ride forward when coming back to collection. When this is possible, the advanced horse is then in front of the leg.

Great care must be taken to ensure that the leg aids are decreased sufficiently to allow the transitions back from extension and medium to collection, or the rider could drive the horse too much into a restraining rein and so lock up his back, causing him to come up against the rein. This is a problem that can be avoided by the rider feeling what is happening to the horse's back and hind steps, and altering the leg and seat aids accordingly. The aids can be given at any time, but the rider must allow the horse to respond to them by having a feeling and assertive arm, leg and seat.

*A Novice horse moving freely
forward from the leg.*

*An Advanced horse moving up
from the leg towards collection.*

Collection

The degree of collection that a horse can produce and maintain throughout his training is an on-going process, that progresses from a minimum amount at Medium level up to the maximum collection and control that has to be shown in the Grand Prix Special test. A top dressage horse must have three good paces, and this collection enhances the paces by developing the rhythm, spring and cadence. If in trying to achieve collection the paces have deteriorated, eg a long-striding walk loses its rhythm, or a springy canter becomes flat when being shortened, then the training is at fault. It is very difficult to re-establish a good walk once it has deteriorated, so great care must be taken when working on this gait.

The advanced horse must be able to show collected, working, medium and extended paces in trot and canter, whereas 'the working walk' is not recognized. However, the free walk on a long rein, where the horse stretches down his neck, has to be shown at the lower levels. The transitions within these gaits should be clear, well defined and without interruption to the outline or the flow of forward movement.

The movements in the dressage tests from Medium to Grand Prix are systematically designed to test the harmony and control that has been developed within the standard of collection that the horse has achieved. Without the necessary collection and correct way of going these movements are of no value, as the combination of the horse and rider performing together should give the impression of having mastered the requirements of each test without difficulty or constraint.

CHAPTER 3

LATERAL
WORK

Lateral work has a very important influence on the horse's education, as it tests his obedience and flexibility to the utmost, and helps to keep all parts of his body supple. It also helps to develop athleticism, control and balance, and therefore helps him contain his impulsion. If left to his natural instincts, this impulsion would normally propel the horse forward at a faster rate, but by increasing the engagement – the ability of the hindquarters to carry more weight – the horse is able to take larger and more powerful steps in extension and shorter, more active, springy steps in collection. Lateral work also helps to develop the horse's mind into an advanced state of obedience and co-operation that allows the rider a higher level of control over the horse's body, enabling him to move the horse both forwards and sideways.

Lateral Exercises

Lateral exercises can be placed under two headings: the preparatory lateral exercises, and the classical lateral movements. The preparatory lateral exercises are the turn about the forehand in walk and leg yielding on a straight line or circle. This is usually done in trot, but can also be performed in walk or canter if the rider feels that it can help solve a specific problem.

The classical lateral movements are the shoulder-in, travers, renvers and half-pass. All these require that the horse moves forward and sideways with a flexion and bend around the rider's inside leg. The more advanced tests require the horse to produce lateral work at a more acute angle. This is only possible when the horse has developed the improved engagement and suppleness required at Advanced level.

At Medium, Advanced Medium, Prix St George and Intermediare I level the shoulder-in is asked for on the centre line or for some distance down either long side of the arena, followed by a turn, circle or transition into medium trot. Travers and renver are rarely asked for in tests but can be ridden in the same place in the arena as shoulder-in.

A lot of importance is placed on the half-pass in all the tests, both in trot and canter. In the Medium, Advanced Medium and Prix St George, the half-passes are executed from the centre line to the outside of the arena and vice versa. At first one change of hand is asked for in the 60m long arena, with each half-pass at a forward angle. As the difficulty increases, several changes of direction are asked for, this movement being known as a zig-zag on the centre line. At Intermediare II, Grand Prix and Grand Prix Special level the half-passes in trot and canter have to be performed all the way across one half of the arena (30m) in either direction. This requires a great deal of collection and engagement, with the horse having to bend and stay in the same rhythm whilst crossing his legs over more in a sideways direction to accommodate the steeper angle.

Flexion and Bend

A horse cannot produce satisfactory lateral work until he is supple enough to bend throughout his body, and some parts have more mobility than others. The head will move to the right or the left at the atlas/axis joint, which is just behind the poll. If the rider can bring the horse's head to the right and see the horse's right eyelashes with a light influence of the right rein, whilst the neck and the rest of the body is kept straight, the horse is said to be flexed to the right. When the horse is flexed in this way he should also 'give' in the jaw, so that the mouth feels soft and submissive to the rein contact. If the lower jaw is tightened and set against the rider's inside rein aid the head could tip; when viewed from the front the horse's face will be tilted, so that the front of the face is no longer vertical. This usually happens if the neck is too short, making the position very uncomfortable for the horse and causing him to lock up his back, inhibiting the use of the hindquarters.

The horse's neck is the easiest section of the spine to bend, so great care must be taken by the rider to ensure that the amount of bend in the neck is under control, as too much will

detract from the correct way of going, allowing the shoulders to escape to the outside of the bend. This will result in horse becoming crooked and therefore not able to 'work through'. Incorrect neck bend is caused by turning the neck too much in the top half, approximately by the fifth or sixth vertebrae from the poll, or alternatively at the base of the neck where it joins the shoulder. Both problems are due to too much influence of the inside rein while not attending to the outside rein, in other words not having the horse correctly between the inside leg and outside rein.

There is very little lateral mobility in the rest of the horse's spine from the withers back to the tail, and in some sections there is none at all. However, with the correct training and development of the horse's muscles and joints he is able to *appear* to bend around the rider's inside leg: science tells us that the horse does not bend its spine from behind the withers

A horse correctly bent around the rider's right leg in shoulder-in (right), and half-pass.

to any degree, yet when correctly trained it feels to the rider and looks to the observer as if the horse is uniformly bent from its poll to its tail.

We cannot explain this apparent contradiction. However, the horse's progressive ability to step sideways and improved mobility of the shoulders, ribcage and hindquarters have an important part to play in this aspect of bending. While still maintaining the spring and suppleness of the horse's movement, these qualities allow the body to look uniformly bent from head to tail even though some parts of the spine will remain straight.

Shoulder-in

For this movement the horse is positioned around the rider's inside leg, with the forehand slightly to the inside of the track being taken by the haunches. If viewed from the front, the horse's hooves can be seen to be on three or four tracks, depending on how much angle the rider asks for. The horse is said to be on three tracks when the inside foreleg makes one track, the outside foreleg and inside hindleg make the second track and the outside hind leg makes the third track. When the angle of the horse's body is further away from the line on which he was originally travelling straight, one track for each leg can be seen distinctly.

The ability to keep the horse straight as his training develops is one of the key factors in reaching a more advanced way of going. Primarily this is achieved by the rider gaining complete control of the horse's shoulders. The horse's desire to escape engaging the hindquarters by becoming crooked increases greatly the more that is asked of him, hence the rider's need to be able to straighten the horse. When a horse is crooked it is possible for the rider to straighten him by placing either the shoulders one way, or the hind-quarters the other.

Experience reveals that to straighten the horse by controlling the hindquarters first is much less efficient than being able to control the shoulders. This is because the hindquarters can become too sensitized to the leg aids, with the result that they will swing excessively from side to side. We therefore straighten the horse by placing the shoulders in front of the hindquarters. Although this is initially more difficult to achieve, it is ultimately more effective. With this in mind, shoulder-in can be said to be the most influential of all lateral movements.

OPPOSITE: *Shoulder-in on three tracks (left), and on four tracks.*

Aids for Shoulder-In

The horse must be prepared for this movement by making sure that the trot is balanced and active. The necessary bend can be acquired through a corner or on a small circle, asking for the flexion with the inside rein and keeping the outside rein to ensure there is not too much neck bend. The inside rein then leads the forehand off the straight line by coming slightly to the inside, while the rider's inside lower leg is used on the girth to push the horse's inside hind leg down the track being taken, at the same time maintaining the bend in his body. The outside leg is used behind the girth to stop the hindquarters swinging out and assists the inside rein in maintaining a constant speed, and also helps to guide the horse to move away from the direction of the bend. Both reins, along with both legs on the girth, are used to straighten the horse once more.

The shoulder-in aids can be used to produce a correct shoulder-in as asked for in the Advanced Medium, Prix St George and Intermediare I tests, or they can be used in trot or canter to place the shoulders slightly to the inside of the haunches in what is called the 'shoulder-fore' position. This is used to correct the outside shoulder when it has bulged out from a straight line. To stop the shoulders deviating from a straight line in canter, the shoulder-in aids are used but without bending the horse's neck.

For test purposes, the movement is ridden with the outside shoulder placed to the inside of the track, so that the outside foreleg is on the same line as the inside hind leg – if viewed from behind the horse would appear to be making three tracks. It is very easy, even with an advanced horse, to produce this position by letting the horse move the hindquarters out rather than by bringing the shoulders in. This may appear the same to the onlooker, but feels very different to the rider and is a serious fault. The horse should be flexed to the inside and be bent uniformly around the rider's inside leg, which is pushing the horse along a line away from the bend; the outside leg is placed behind the girth to control the hindquarters and therefore help to keep the bend. The horse's inside hind leg takes an increased share of the weight and should step well underneath the body as it does so, If the horse works correctly in shoulder-in without losing impulsion and suppleness, the collection will be improved and, because of this increased engagement, so will the horse's ability to move forward into medium and extended gaits without losing balance.

Further Uses for Shoulder-In

The shoulder-in is used mostly in trot, but can usefully be employed in walk as a preparation before walk pirouettes, or to straighten the horse if he has a tendency to fall on to either shoulder in anticipation of performing rein back or piaffe. It can also be used to correct straightness during these movements. In addition, it is especially useful in canter to straighten the horse before a movement is executed up the centre line or on the long sides of the arena. It is also a good preparation for canter pirouettes, and is used extensively when riding the counter changes of hand (or zig-zag). Here the shoulder-in is used after each flying change to position the horse before progressing in half-pass in the new direction.

If the horse feels stiff on a 10m or 8m circle, first work on a larger circle and ride him forward, encouraging him to lower his neck to stretch and loosen the topline. This should be followed by some transitions from trot to walk or a very slow trot, and then forward again in a more active trot until he is carrying himself well. Then work the horse in shoulder-in on the circle to engage the hind legs and encourage the bend that is needed for the smaller circles. Spiralling in to an 8m circle from shoulder-in on a 20m circle will often help to keep the collection and suppleness that so easily fades away on small circles.

Difficulties and Corrections

The supreme test of controlling shoulder-in in trot is to execute it on the centre line. Without the support of the wall of the school the horse will at first feel unbalanced and wobbly, and has to be bent securely around the rider's inside leg and working confidently into the rider's hand before he will manage it fluently. He must, of course, start the movement by bringing the shoulders to the inside and not by swinging the hindquarters out. If a circle is made off the centre line and shoulder-in is asked for on regaining the line, the same technique applies.

Ten-metre circles are a very revealing way to test the suppleness and impulsion before or after any movement. In both instances they must be flowing, rhythmic and look easy, with the horse remaining active. If head tipping occurs during this exercise it usually signifies there is either a non-acceptance of the rein or the rider has the rein too strong. The horse must allow the rider to apply the aids with a soft contact on the mouth.

RIGHT: *Shoulder-in position with very little bend.*

FAR RIGHT: *Shoulder-in with active working trot steps, showing more bend in the neck than the body.*

If after riding the shoulder-in the horse feels as if he is lacking in impulsion, he must be ridden well forward into a stronger trot on either a 20m circle or a straight line. This will freshen up the trot, and the horse can then be asked to make shoulder-in again in a more forward-going manner. If allowed, a lazy horse will use the lateral work to disengage his hindquarters, and exercises in leg yielding, and shoulder-in on a large circle in a freer trot, will help substantiate the forward movement, which is essential in order to prevent the collection from diminishing. Impulsion is inclined to ebb in all lateral work and care must be taken, by alternating the sideways movements with medium and extended exercises, that this does not become a habit.

Too much angle in the shoulder-in will make it difficult for the horse to maintain impulsion, and too much bend in the neck will allow him to fall on to the outside shoulder rather than engage the inside hind leg. These examples of the main problems that can be encountered when riding shoulder-in signify that if not ridden correctly there will be no benefits from this exercise.

Travers

For this movement the horse's hindquarters are moved to the inside of the track, so that the horse is slightly bent around the rider's inside leg. The horse is bent in the direction of the movement, and the angle and bend throughout should be the same as that shown in shoulder-in.

Travers is the first movement in trot that really tests the bend of the horse around the rider's inside leg, because now he is required to move in the direction of that bend. If the horse is not supple, not engaged behind or is disobedient to the leg aids, he will not be able to perform a fluent travers.

The weight-carrying capacity of the inside hind leg is increased dramatically in this movement, because when the hindquarters are moved in from the track the horse's body weight moves sideways, and the outside fore and hind legs cross over in front of the inside pair, causing the inside hind to bear extra weight. Because of this it is a valuable movement for increasing collection in both trot and canter, and for testing the horse's obedience and capacity to maintain the bend under more difficult circumstances than previously required. The horse can be positioned for travers on a straight line or on a circle.

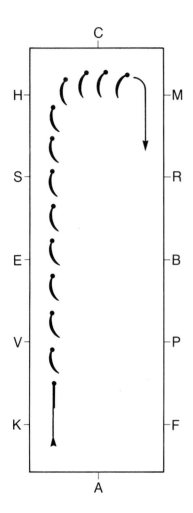

Travers in canter on the inside track of the arena and making a half-circle at the end of the arena.

Aids for Travers

Before giving the aids for travers, the rider must prepare the trot by checking the balance and impulsion and producing sufficient flexion for travers on a small circle or corner. The rider's outside leg behind the girth pushes the hindquarters to the inside, whilst pressure from the inside lower leg maintains the forward movement and gives the horse a support to bend around. The inside rein prevents the horse looking to the outside and keeps a degree of flexion, while the outside rein controls the speed and prevents too much bend in the neck. The horse should be ridden out of this position from the inside leg into the outside rein.

When travers is performed against the wall of the school, it is easier to control the horse's shoulders. However, as with the shoulder-in, when it is asked for up the centre line there is a greater test of control, and the ability to keep the horse's front feet on the line during several changes from travers left to travers right and vice versa is a good preparation before attempting the counter change of hand (the changing of direction within the half-pass).

Half-pass

The half-pass is a more difficult variation of travers, as it is executed along a diagonal line as opposed to the straight wall or the centre line of the school. Travers on a volte (6m circle), is known as a pasade. When performed in canter, this exercise is a good preparation for the canter pirouette.

These two exercises are very similar so there is no difference in the rider's aids for travers or half-pass. The horse must be very obedient to the outside leg, which moves the horse sideways at the desired angle, while at the same time the inside leg maintains the impulsion and keeps the bend and direction asked for with the inside rein. The amount of bend in the horse's neck is controlled with the outside rein. For half-pass, the rider has to have a sophisticated control of the horse's shoulders.

If the horse's reaction to the inside leg is not good, he will be inclined to push weight on to his inside shoulder, lessening the bend in his body and therefore avoiding engaging his inside hind leg. In order to proceed at the correct angle he must move forward readily from the inside leg, while remaining bent around it.

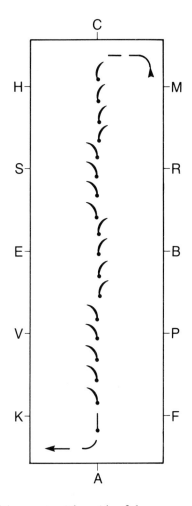

Travers to either side of the centre line: an exercise in trot for changing the bend alternately. Viewed from the front, it should look the same each way.

RIGHT: *Here the shoulders are in the correct position, slightly in front of the hindquarters. However, there is little bend in this half-pass left.*

CENTRE: *This shows more bend, but the shoulders have been left slightly behind. When viewed from the front, the hindquarters will be leading.*

FAR RIGHT: *Here the shoulders have regained the correct position.*

RIGHT: *In this half-pass the hindquarters are being forced over without the shoulder foremost. The result is discomfort and some head tipping.*

FAR RIGHT: *The rider has now corrected the position and is showing a good half-pass right.*

Renvers

Renvers is a further variation of this position, using identical aids to half-pass and travers. The hindquarters stay on the track, with the forehand to the inside at the same angle as the travers or shoulder-in. The bend of the horse and the rider's inside leg is now to the outside of the school, with the horse moving in the direction in which he is bent. This movement is called 'tail to the wall' as opposed to travers, which is called 'head to the wall'.

Using Lateral Work in Trot

Lateral movements can be used to improve the horse's obedience to the aids. The horse will also benefit from the increased mobility and suppleness within the collected trot, and this is especially true if the rider exercises the horse by riding alternately from one movement to the other. For example, ride shoulder-in for 20m, and then circle 8m and go directly into travers.

It is useful to position the horse in renvers after making some half-pass, particularly if the horse has collapsed back to the track without being able to maintain the correct bend. In this case, put the horse into renvers 2m before reaching the track and ride on down the side of the school, keeping the horse placed around the inside leg, as he should have been in the half-pass.

It is more desirable that the horse should be correctly bent and step sideways with adequate collection, showing a large, springy stride with the hindquarters trailing slightly, than stay strictly parallel to the wall showing less or no bend and an inhibited stride.

For training purposes, so long as the bend is maintained, it can be helpful to place the horse's shoulders deliberately well in advance of the hindquarters to ensure that the shoulders are moving freely.

However, if the bend and impulsion are not kept because the horse has lost his balance, his weight will fall on to the inside shoulder, the carrying power of the hindquarters will be lost and the resulting effect will be that of a straight horse falling sideways. If the position of the half-pass has been lost in trot, it is possible to re-establish it by riding some shoulder-in or travers to gain acceptance of the aids, alternating these movements with some medium trot to restore any loss of impulsion.

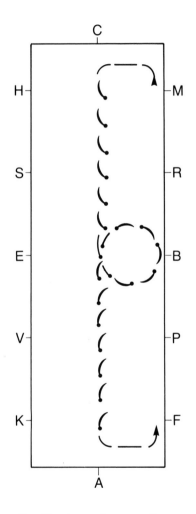

Shoulder-in on the centre line into a 10m circle, then into travers.

Using Lateral Work in Canter

In canter I prefer to make renvers as opposed to travers on the wall, since it is always difficult to have the horse absolutely straight on the long side of the arena as he likes to hug the wall with his outside shoulder. This will then make it easier for the inside hind leg to come through to the inside of the foreleg, which will result in the horse being crooked. To ask for travers in this situation is to encourage this tendency.

I prefer to ask for travers in canter on a large or small circle or anywhere away from the track. This encourages weight on to the inside hind leg and an increased bending of the joints. If travers is asked for in canter, an equivalent amount of shoulder-fore should be maintained afterwards in order to ensure that the horse allows himself to be straightened easily after having the hindquarters to the inside. If the bend is not sufficient in canter, 10m or smaller circles will help to establish it, so long as the rider's inside leg is used efficiently.

Another useful exercise is to rider travers along the three-quarter line, then keeping it on a half circle and again up the three-quarter line on the other side of the school, to help establish the bend and acceptance of the movement (see the diagram on page 54).

Half-Pass in Canter

When viewed from in front, the horse executing half-pass should be bent around the rider's inside leg as in travers, but with the shoulders stepping marginally in advance of the hindquarters towards the direction of movement. The horse's body remains more or less parallel to the long side and there should not be an excessive bend in the neck, as this inhibits the flow and stride from the inside shoulder. Instead, the neck should curve gently towards the required marker, with the flexion corresponding to the position of the whole horse and not exaggerated, with too much turning of the head a the top of the neck. This position should look identical to right or left and is the same for both trot and canter. Half-pass in passage is not a movement that is required in the present international dressage tests, but it is shown by some competitors as a non-compulsory addition to add effect and flair to their Freestyle to Music programme.

It is easier to keep the horse bent around the riders' inside leg in canter than it is in trot. The horse is naturally bent to the leading leg in canter and so the canter half-pass is a simpler movement than the trot half-pass. Canter half-pass

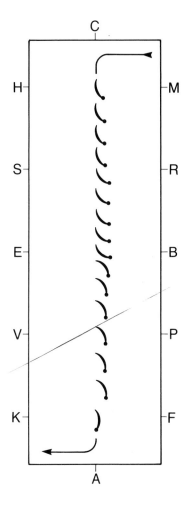

Shoulder-in into renvers, keeping the hind steps on the centre line but changing the bend, and moving first away from the bend and then into it.

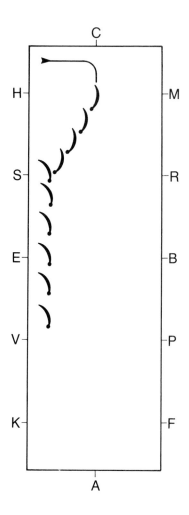

Half-pass into renvers in trot or canter right.

This horse has his nose a little behind the vertical. However, he is supple and showing the correct bend for canter half-pass left.

across the whole diagonal in a 20 × 60m arena can be executed in a forward-going and free canter to loosen up the horse and get him moving forward as well as sideways: the more acute the angle that is asked for in any half-pass the more collected and engaged the horse has to be. Always start with an easy angle in both trot and canter, making sure that the horse moves sideways in the correct position before asking for a more acute line.

Difficulties and Corrections

When a horse is unwilling to offer the necessary bend in either of the half-passes, the rider is often justified in coming back to walk to work on loosening the neck and establishing that the horse is willing and able to accept the bend, before returning to the trot and the canter. Lack of bend is usually due to the rider failing to prepare correctly for the movement. If the horse tends to run away from the outside leg, going forwards instead of willingly moving sideways, then the extra impulsion in trot and canter makes the movement more difficult than in walk. Often this problem results in a shortening of the neck as the rider attempts to control the speed. When the neck gets short and tight it is more difficult and unpleasant for the horse to bend around the riders' inside leg, and a situation of resistance and stiffness develops. This should be avoided by establishing the suppleness and flexibility at an easier level and then gradually building up to a more difficult degree of bend and engagement. The horse should not be held into the bend with a forceful rein. If this were to happen the steps and flow of the movement would be greatly impaired. If to position a difficult horse the rein aid has to be a little stronger than desired, it should be lightened as soon as the position is established and the horse must then be allowed to obey the sideways leg aid without any constriction from the rein. The horse must be trained to accomplish all lateral work in a flowing manner without the reins becoming any stronger than normal.

A useful exercise to help maintain the bend in the trot half-pass is to do a 'zig-zag' of leg yielding and half-passes, either from the centre line or round the outside track of the arena. Use the leg yielding to push the horse around the inside leg and to keep him moving forward, so that when moving back into a half-pass the inside leg will prevent him falling on to his inside shoulder and thus possibly eliminating the bend.

This pushing on to the inside shoulder is the most common fault in half-pass and is usually a result of the rider

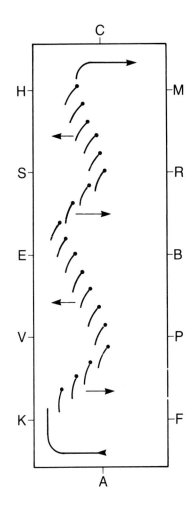

Half-pass into leg yielding round the outside of the arena.

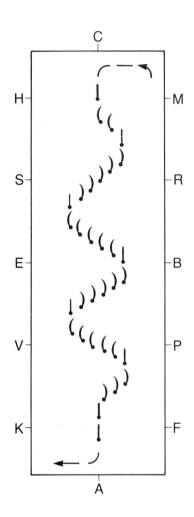

A Grand Prix zig-zag in canter.

failing to use sufficient inside leg aids whilst riding the movement, or using too much outside rein instead of enough outside leg. The other fault that can occur specifically in the half-pass is that of the hindquarters leading or trailing. In either case the rider has to become aware of this feeling and correct the fault as soon as it occurs, by gaining more control of the shoulders and placing them in the correct position.

Counter Change of Hand

The counter change of hand (or zig-zag) is a movement which incorporates the half-pass. In trot the distance travelled sideways is measured in metres, while in canter it is measured by the number of canter strides. In either case it involves a half-pass to the left followed by a half-pass to the right (or vice versa).

The degree of difficulty is dependent on the steepness of the angle of each half pass and how many changeovers are required. In the Advanced Medium test the collected trot half-pass is 5m to the left, 10m to the right and then 5m back to the left, while in the Grand Prix test five counter changes of hand in collected canter are required. The first half-pass to the left and the last to the right are both of three strides and the four others are of six strides. The criterion by which this movement is assessed is the control of the shoulders during the changeover from one direction to the other, providing the half-pass is correct between the changes of direction and the collection is maintained.

In trot

To make a correct changeover from half-pass left to half-pass right in trot, the rider must ensure that the hindquarters are not trailing at the moment before the changeover occurs. The horse must first be straightened before the shoulders, head and neck are positioned to the right in preparation for the correct half-pass in the new direction. When introducing the horse to this movement, it is advisable not to ride an accurate changeover at a specific place, but to take time using as many steps as necessary to straighten and reposition the horse. When the horse understands what is wanted and can make the changeover in walk or trot in three steps – one step being used to straighten the horse, and two to establish the shoulder-fore position before moving sideways – that is the time to start making an accurate change of hand at X. In the 20 × 60m arena, half-pass is ridden from K to X and then a

The photographs on this page and page 66 show the horse changing the bend in a counter change of hand.

LEFT: *Half-pass left in collected canter.*

RIGHT: *Straightening the horse before making the flying change.*

LEFT: *Landing from the flying change and looking to the right.*

RIGHT: *Moving into half-pass right with the correct bend and position.*

change of hand before returning back to the track at H. The changeover should be arranged so that the horse leaves the X marker having made the new position. This means that the rider must reach the centre line three steps before X in order to accomplish the accuracy needed to prevent the X–H line becoming too steep.

When the horse can make a good changeover from either rein, the next step is an easy zig-zag down the centre line. This entails 5m to the left in half-pass, followed by 10m to the right, ending with 5m back to the left before continuing on down the centre line. During this type of movement the

rhythm and quality of the trot must remain constant, and the horse should not tip his head or set his jaw when asked to bend in either direction. It is important that the rider keeps his weight well down into the inside stirrup and does not get left behind the movement during the changes of direction.

The Grand Prix and Intermediare II tests do not contain a difficult counter change of hand in trot. In fact, only one changeover is asked for in the Intermediare II: the difficulty lies in maintaining the required acute angle of half-pass all the way across the arena without losing the collection and cadence that make this movement so attractive.

This horse is taking extravagant steps to the right with a sufficient bend, while keeping the rhythm and quality of the trot.

67

In canter

The counter change of hand in canter is a more difficult movement and establishing it in trot first will help, as the technique and control needed for positioning the shoulders is very similar. Counting the steps as the leading leg reaches the ground and incorporating a flying change during this positioning makes the movement more complicated to ride.

The horse must be very steady and established in the changes before attempting this type of work and, as in trot, accuracy is not the first consideration when training. The control of the shoulders is paramount and therefore time can be taken in the early stages to straighten the horse after one half-pass, make the flying change, and then position the horse for the new half-pass, before starting to count the steps and worry about riding the movement as required in a test.

In canter, just as in trot, it is important that the hindquarters are not trailing before making the flying change, and I like to push them over so that the horse is exactly parallel to the centre line before giving the change aid. As soon as the new leading leg has touched the ground before starting the new half-pass, the horse must be put in a slight shoulder-in position.

Difficulties and Corrections

Useful exercises to help gain control and prepare for the counter change of hand are either to make a simple instead of a flying change and use the walk steps to reposition the horse's shoulders, before striking off to the new lead and half-pass, or to start counting the steps in the half-pass – say eight – ride forward with the neck absolutely straight for a few strides, and then ride a further eight steps of half-pass. This helps the inexperienced rider to start counting the steps and prepares the horse for the greater flexibility needed to take a few steps one way, alter the position, and take a few steps in the opposite direction.

However, it is difficult for the horse to maintain collection while learning this movement, as there is a tendency for the weight to fall on to the shoulders during the flying change and change of direction. If the weight does fall on to the forehand, it is better to rebalance the horse on a 10m circle, making the necessary transitions and half-halts, and to freshen up the canter with some longer strides, before continuing with the half-passes once again.

There is nothing to be gained by making this movement without the necessary balance, suppleness and collection.

The rider should always be prepared to 'back pedal' when things go wrong and assess the progress in a constructive way, so that corrections can be made before the horse establishes habits that are difficult to cure.

If when cantering in half-pass at an Advanced Medium angle the horse has not been trained to show an equal bend to the right and to the left from the centre line to the outside track, he is not going to show an equal bend while making the simplest counter change of hand, and it is pointless to progress to the more difficult movement until the easier one has been perfected.

Advanced Zig-zag in Trot

As the horse progresses and is asked to make the longer and more steeply angled half-passes required in the more advanced tests, the rider can have a lot of influence on reducing the difficulty of the movement by correct preparation and how and when he starts it.

For example, if you start a half-pass to the left at F which has to go all the way across the arena to E and then back in right half-pass to M, you must arrive at the track a little before E so that the changeover can be made giving as much room as possible for the second half-pass, making it less difficult than if it had started after the E marker. It is vital to prepare for the first half-pass by positioning the horse around your inside leg in the corner of the arena and to leave the track as soon as the horse's shoulders reach the marker. I like to push the horse well sideways for the first two or three steps while there is still plenty of impulsion available, and then carefully plan a line that finishes at the opposite track two or three strides before the E marker. The second half-pass is usually more difficult, as the impulsion can diminish unless the horse is extremely athletic and supple, and finds it easy to maintain the necessary impulsion for such a long session of sideways movement. It is therefore important to keep the shoulder free to take big steps to the side without too much bend in the neck, and also to make sure that the hindquarters do not trail.

Most horses find this movement easier in canter than in trot, provided they are able to produce adequate collection and sideways movement. The larger and springier the sideways steps, the more impressive the movement appears and the easier it is to ride. Nothing looks worse than a long line of half-pass with the horse stepping sideways, having lost the moment of suspension in the trot or the canter.

The Grand Prix Zig-Zag in Canter

The judge expects to see a few steps of straight canter before the start and at the end of this movement, which is meant to be completed at the G marker. If the horse is not sufficiently collected and therefore inclined to canter too freely, there is not enough room to fit the movement into the 50m of the centre line available.

There should be three uniform strides on either side of the centre line all the way down the arena, and at this level the horse is straightened out on the sixth stride and positioned for the new direction during the flying change, so that the first stride of the new canter shows the correct degree of angle and flow required. It helps if the horse's neck can be straightened the stride before his body is put into the new position, as this makes for a smoother picture when viewed from the front. The horse is also less likely to be thrown off balance by a sharp change of the neck position.

Precision in this movement can be practised by cantering round the track of the arena and making six half-pass strides away from the track and a flying change, before making six strides back to the track. The horse will often find it easier to cover the ground to one side than he does to the other, and this exercise is a beneficial way of assessing whether the steps are equal to the right and left. It should, therefore, be practised on both the right and left rein.

The horse will usually cover more ground to his soft side than to his stiff side. The rider's weight, correctly placed into the inside stirrup, will always encourage the horse to make good sideways steps, and any tendency to take the inside rein away from the line of movement and draw it back over the withers, in order to maintain the bend and control the shoulders, should be avoided. The inside shoulder should be controlled by the inside leg only and the reins should be short enough to produce the correct flexion and neck position, and thereafter ride the movement with a good-quality connection. To maintain this flexion, only the outside leg should be used to take the hindquarters over, not the outside rein.

Whatever lateral work is being shown, it will only be of good quality and deserve a high mark if the collection is well maintained, the rhythm remains unaltered and there is a willing acceptance of the rider's hand throughout. To test this ideal state of control, the rider should be able to give away the inside rein, or the outside rein, or both reins, during the half-pass in trot or canter, without the horse losing the correct position or the balance.

CHAPTER 4

FLYING CHANGES

The flying change is a movement whereby the horse changes the canter lead during the moment of suspension when all four feet are off the ground *without* losing the canter sequence. It therefore goes without saying that before being able to make big and impressive flying changes, the horse must have developed a good three-beat canter which has a clear moment of suspension. However, it is just as possible for a horse to change from a canter that is flat and lacks any expression, although the changes themselves will then also possess these undesirable qualities.

The actual process of teaching the horse to make a flying change must be carefully thought out, because if the technique is not efficient the horse can acquire the habit of changing with the foreleg one or more strides before the hind leg, which can be a difficult problem to overcome. If the horse makes this error it is termed as being 'late behind'. If not corrected, the horse is then said to be cantering 'disunited'. However, the opposite can also occur and the change can be 'late in front', which is when the hind leg comes through before the front leg. This is not such a serious problem, as it usually means that the rein is too strong and when the horse is put in better balance and stops leaning on the rein, the change is usually correct.

A change that is late behind is caused by a variety of problems such as lack of impulsion, lack of position (crookedness of the horse), stiffness, the horse not being on the aids, or just a misunderstanding of what is required. An athletic horse does not have to be collected to make flying changes, but a stiff horse, with only a moderate canter, must be well towards showing a shorter, more collected canter in order to achieve the correct result. This is because his natural

A Grand Prix horse cantering during a training session. Following the moment of suspension the near hind has come to the ground, the off hind and near fore are almost to the ground together, and the off fore is coming through as the leading leg and will finish the sequence of steps when it comes to the ground – then the moment of suspension will occur once more.

gait does not enable him to make a fluent change and so, for example, if he were loose in a paddock or indoor school his flying changes would probably be naturally late behind. The horse's training must have developed so that he can canter correctly in order to produce the changes in an easy manner. An athletic horse will make correct changes naturally, but can also find it very easy to canter disunited.

When choosing a potential dressage horse it is always an advantage to see the horse loose in a suitable enclosure. This will enable you to assess the horse's ability and desire to make flying changes.

Aids for Flying Changes

The horse should not be asked to make a flying change until he is able to strike off into canter on either leg from trot or walk in any position that the rider demands. For example, the horse should be able to make simple changes on a circle, a simple change from a counter-canter figure-of-eight, and serpentines with changes through either trot or walk. Another useful exercise is to rider canter to walk and walk to canter around the outside track of the arena on either rein, not always changing the lead but making random strike offs into canter. To be absolutely fluent in these exercises will ensure that the horse knows, without any shadow of a doubt, the rider's leg aids for canter left or right. It will also teach him that he must not anticipate the flying change, but wait for the correct signal before changing.

A horse well engaged in canter left, with the near hind stepping well under the body. This canter is suitable for making a flying change.

ABOVE AND RIGHT: *A well-balanced counter canter with the near fore as the leading leg. The rider's right leg is slightly behind the girth, signifying to the horse to stay in canter left. This horse looks ready and attentive enough to make a flying change.*

The aid given by the rider for the flying change is exactly the same as the aid for canter that was taught to the horse when he was a novice and was asked to strike off into canter right or canter left from trot. In basic terms, the flying change is merely asking for either canter right or canter left from the opposite lead whilst remaining in canter. For the change to be correct, the horse must change the sequence during the moment of suspension, so that the new inside hind and foreleg can come to the ground in the correct order.

The rider can give the aid for canter strike off with either the inside or the outside leg. Training systems round the world vary and it is quite correct to use either method. Personally, I prefer to maintain impulsion with the inside leg and ask for a canter strike off or for a flying change with the outside leg, and will therefore refer to this method.

Trainers and competition riders will vary slightly in their

application of the aid for the flying change. It is not important how far back or forward the rider's legs are put to ask for the change, or whether the horse changes as the leg is stroked back or simply waits for a nudge from the rider's leg behind the girth, as long as the horse understands the aid and is properly prepared. It is important that the aid is given at the appropriate moment so that the horse has time to recognize the aid and react during the moment of suspension of the canter. It would be very confusing for the horse if he had been trained to canter from the outside leg and then a different rider asked for changes with the inside leg.

The most important and skilful preparation involves having the correct qualities in the canter and the ability to feel whether or not the horse is straight, is in a good position for the change and is also calm and relaxed. By this I mean that when you first teach a young horse changes he must stay relaxed, round, and good in the hand. Even if there is an element of tension these criteria are important, otherwise the change could be 'late behind', a situation which should be avoided if at all possible. Therefore, when the horse is first learning flying changes, the rider must stay calm and re-establish a relaxed way of going as soon as possible after the initial upset, which is quite normal.

Starting to Teach Flying Changes

The best time to start work on flying changes is when there is a lull in the competition routine, as the quality of the canter may be affected by the horse anticipating a flying change. A horse which is collecting points that will put him out of the Medium level must be confirmed and established in the changes before competing at Advanced Medium. If the necessary homework has been done at a time during the previous winter when it does not matter if the counter canter becomes a little fragile or the normal canter rather tense because the horse is learning to change legs, it will stand the horse in good stead for the more continuous work on this exercise. If the canter is good enough, the talented horse can learn flying changes while he is still competing at Elementary level. Once the horse has mastered a skill he will never forget the process, even if he has not been asked for six months or more – such is the trainability of the horse's mind.

The rider can start asking for changes when he feels that the horse is cantering with enough impulsion and can remain in balance, be straightened with the shoulder-in aids without bending the neck (in fact, the horse must allow his head and neck to be placed away from the leading leg in canter if the rider wishes to take the weight off the outside shoulder before making a change), and understands the aids to canter left or right.

When teaching flying changes to a young horse or Thoroughbred type with a sensitive back, I adopt a light seat to lessen the weight on the seat bones, putting more weight on the knee and thigh, in order that the horse does not feel inhibited by the rider's weight and learns to make a big, springy change of leg. It is important that the flying change strides are as long as or longer than the canter stride. If they are shorter or do not come through at all (almost resembling a 'bunny jump', with both hind legs coming to the ground together) the rider must check that the impulsion and roundness of the horse are sufficient and that the horse has not become tight in the back due to the tension of learning a new exercise. He must be ridden actively forward to freshen up the canter and be asked to change from a less collected canter to encourage the hind leg to come through. This problem can also be improved by working the horse in a field with good going. The rider should shorten his stirrups and lighten his seat and ask for some changes in a more forward canter, while keeping the horse well balanced and correctly working into his hands.

Initially it does not matter if the horse is crooked, hollows or gets generally tight when making the change – the main requirement is that he must learn to change to the new canter lead. If he only changes in front when first asked, at least he has done something in response to the leg aid; it is often the case that a sharper and stronger leg aid is needed to emphasize that something must happen both in front and behind. The horse's temperament when learning the changes has a large influence on how the rider conducts the work. The nervous and highly strung horse must be kept as relaxed as possible, walking to calm him down when necessary. A phlegmatic and less sensitive horse may at first have to be made a little agitated as well as activated, to get the desired result. The leg aid must be given in a stronger, clearer way and if it is ignored the stick may have to be used as a back-up. The degree of tension that is common with this type of reaction may help the rider to achieve what is wanted.

When teaching the horse flying changes, or when perfecting them, it is advisable to have a person on the ground who is experienced in observing the horse changing legs, because it is not always possible for the rider to feel if the change is late behind, particularly if the horse has a smooth canter. It is important that an incorrect change should be attempted again to ascertain whether it is possible to make it correct. It is also vital to make a fuss of the horse the moment that he has understood what he is supposed to do and to praise him when he has tried to oblige.

Some horses, especially the Thoroughbred type, can get very excited at first, and in this case it helps to keep them calm by walking them after each change and to wait until they have relaxed before cantering again. Warmbloods are usually far more temperate about this part of their education and will normally learn the change from either canter lead without any difficulty. However, at the beginning most horses find it easier to change one way than the other. Having established which is the more harmonious side, it is a

1

2

The sequence of photographs on these two pages shows clearly what happens when the horse makes a flying change from canter left to canter right. As the change is made the croup has lifted, possibly due to resentment of the aid or not moving forward sufficiently. However, the horse remains round, straight and on the bit.

3

4

5

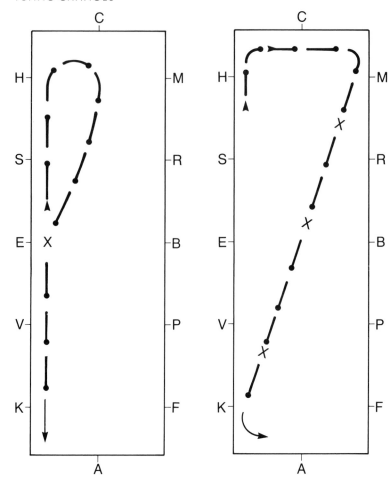

LEFT: *X marks the place to ask for a flying change for the first time, from canter right to canter left.*

RIGHT: *X marks the place on the diagonal to make three flying changes when first starting sequence changes.*

good idea to leave the more difficult side until the horse is really fluent and confident to the aids, and then progress to establishing the change to the more difficult side. I have found that when learning changes horses are very like left- or right-handed people and the rider must make allowances for this.

The most suitable place in the arena first to ask for a flying change is somewhere on the second half of a diagonal line across the arena before turning into the corner, or alternatively to make half a 10m circle and then progress back to the track, making the change when the horse is positioned and feels ready. At first, horses will anticipate the movement and will often throw in changes without being asked. They must not be punished or reprimanded for doing this, as they are only trying to please. Eventually, an understanding between the horse and rider must be established, so that even though the horse knows a flying change is needed, he must learn to wait for the rider to tell him exactly when to change, and the rider's leg will position and hold the horse in one canter lead until the new canter lead is asked for. With an exuberant horse this is easier said than done, particularly at the beginning, but the rider will learn to feel how the horse is reacting and if he is anticipating a change, and be able to keep the horse in counter canter. Do no make too many changes in the same place unless the horse is being a little slow on the uptake or unwilling, in which case using repetition at the same place will create anticipation and some tension, which in these circumstances will help produce a change. Riding a shallow loop in from the side of the school and then making a flying change to the outside is often a good way of stopping a horse anticipating, as it is not so easy to change to the outside in the initial stages.

The aids to hold the horse in canter to the leading leg, and so prevent him throwing in a change without being asked, are the same as positioning for the shoulder-fore but without bending the neck. This position is used continually in all the canter exercises to control the horse's shoulders and therefore keep the horse straight. Being able to establish the angle of this shoulder-fore position, even though it is very slight, is most important, particularly before a change – or during a change if the hindquarters are swinging – and then immed-iately after a change. The ability to control the shoulders during the tempi changes, which are changes every four strides, three strides, two strides and ultimately every stride, is especially important.

Riding a Sequence of Changes

It is not advisable to start asking for more than a single flying change until the horse is really calm, stays round and straight, remains in a good canter rhythm and can make flying changes anywhere that he is asked in the arena. When this can be achieved, it is the right time to start asking for changes on a related number of canter strides.

It is best to start by riding two or three changes every six strides down one long side of the arena, and then three changes across the diagonal – one off the first corner, one at X, and the third just before the quarter marker at the end of the diagonal. When this can be done without tension, four-time changes can be attempted. If the horse gets very excited and is inclined to increase speed and then become strong in

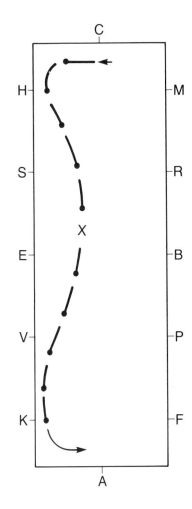

X marks the place on a loop down the long side of the arena to ask for a flying change from the inside to the outside – a good place when the young horse is anticipating changes.

the hand, the rider must be tactful and not put too many changes together in the early stages. Using the last part of the diagonal line to make a change every four strides is less exciting than starting the flying changes at the beginning. Likewise, the second half of the long side of the arena before walking in the corner will also be less exciting. A horse will usually get tired of running away if he is asked to make a pasade each time he does, encouraging the weight back on to the hindquarters and obtaining more balance. It is most important that the rein does not become too strong during

A horse showing shoulder-fore in canter right, a position that is used while preparing the horse for flying changes or to control the shoulders.

the sequence changes, as this will result in their being flat and dull. Instead, the energy that the horse puts into going too fast must be utilized to encourage him to spring off the ground, showing large and impressive changes which the judges will reward with high marks.

When four-time changes present no difficulties, three- and two-time sequences may be started. These are not usually a problem if the earlier work is well confirmed. A satisfactory introduction can be made by asking for three changes on every third stride starting with the right canter lead, coming back to walk and patting the horse before doing the same again but this time starting with the left canter lead. The same method should be used when asking for changes every second stride, so that the horse does not become upset by being asked for a longer series in a sequence that he is not used to. Gradually increase the number of changes, but only if the horse remains straight and relaxed. If the horse becomes strong in the hand or the changes are not fluent, return to the easier work until the horse is better prepared.

When riding the sequence changes across the diagonal in a test, it is important to prepare the horse in the corner before turning on to the diagonal. Always check the balance, especially if the previous movement has been an extended canter, by making a half-halt and at the same time position the horse in shoulder-fore so that the turn on to the diagonal is straight, with the shoulders well under control and the horse in front of the rider's inside leg.

Do not start the changes too early or too late. Plan to make the change in the middle of the sequence over the X marker. For example, if five changes every four strides are asked for, the third change should be on the X marker. This gives a symmetrical look to the movement and shows the judge that the rider is in complete control. Young horses starting sequence changes will at times drift to one side, usually the stiff side. It may be possible to keep the horse's body straight, although this can be difficult at this stage. If you know the horse is going to make ground to the right, for example, when changing the rein from the left to the right while making some changes on the diagonal, it helps to ride well to the left of the marker at the end of the diagonal, so that there is no danger of cutting the corner and unbalancing the horse further. As the horse becomes accustomed to maintaining his balance during the changes, the rider will not have to make such allowances as it will be easier to keep on a straight line, whether it be the diagonal or the centre line.

1

The sequence of photographs on these two pages shows the horse landing in canter right while making two-time changes. Note that the rider's right leg is forward whilst the left has asked for the change. Having made a step in canter right, the rider's right leg moves back to ask for canter left, and so on. The horse remains straight and calm.

2

3

4

Difficulties and Corrections

Swinging Hindquarters

Many horses will swing their hindquarters from side to side when they make the changes, and if this is obvious when riding across the diagonal during the tempi changes, it will be marked down accordingly. The aim of the rider should be to have established a fluent and straight single change before starting to teach tempi changes. To do this, the change must be made without the horse hollowing and drawing back from the rider's hand, losing impulsion, or coming croup high and therefor plunging down on to the forehand. The aid for the flying change should be made as the horse's leading leg comes forward, so that he can organize his legs during the moment of suspension and bring the two legs on the new inside forward without losing rhythm or forward momentum.

If the horse swings his hindquarters to the right as he changes from left to right, the cause is often that the rider is using too much right rein to indicate that a change is wanted, instead of keeping the new outside rein (in this case the left) to prevent the horse's weight falling on to the left shoulder. As in all the other movements, control of the shoulders is vital, and if the rider concentrates on keeping the shoulders on line and riding the horse forward with a good rein contact, the hindquarters will stop swinging and follow through on that straight line. The rider must sit very quietly while giving the change aid, and avoid the temptation to throw the weight over to either side to encourage the horse to change legs. If the rider's inside hip is collapsed when the outside leg gives the aid for the change, the rider's weight will fall to the outside and unbalance the horse, making further changes difficult as well as making the changes looking unco-ordinated and ungraceful. Ideally, the rider should sit very quietly in the saddle and it should not be obvious to the onlooker when the new inside seat bone allows the new inside leg to come through.

Running Away from the Leg

It is also possible when teaching the flying change to come across the situation where instead of trying to change legs, the horse merely runs away from the leg aid. This can often be the case with a small rider on a large horse, when the problem may have to be rectified by putting an experienced and stronger jockey aboard until the horse makes a change and ceases to run off.

It is important that the rider puts the horse in a good position in this situation to make it easy for the horse to change, and vital that the new inside rein is kept light as the new leading leg comes through. This is not easily done if the horse has been pulling up to the moment of asking, so it is important to stress that the canter must be balanced and the horse obedient before working on the flying changes.

It may take several months to get the horse accustomed to the leg aids and obeying them before the changes themselves can be straightened, with the horse staying round and in good rhythm. Cantering out in a big field can often be beneficial in helping to establish the rhythm and get the horse over the worry of having to change at various intervals from straight lines, circles or counter canter, the added space being useful either to settle the horse or to cultivate more impulsion as the need arises.

As the horse gains confidence in making the changes, the work can progress to incorporating them into different movements. The ability to cope with this varies enormously with each horse: one horse will be able to make a canter serpentine and change legs over the centre line, change to the outside on a large circle, and start sequence changes all in a matter of weeks, whereas a more highly strung horse may take a year or more to settle down and make one single flying change in a calm and confident manner. The sensitive horse can create difficulties for the rider, who must be extremely patient and laid back with this type of horse, his attitude remaining calm to cope with the horse's nervousness.

Changing 'Late Behind'

Another problem which is quite common is when the horse continually changes with the hind leg coming through one stride late behind. This often happens when an inexperienced rider teaches the horse flying changes. Once it is a confirmed habit it can be difficult to correct, and an experienced trainer may have to assess the problem, improve the canter with more impulsion and balance, and position the horse carefully to make it easier for a correct change to come through. In this situation the emphasis must be on making a correct change, and if this has to be from an accentuated shoulder-in position, from travers or from extra collection then so be it. Later on, when the correct changes are confirmed, the horse must be made straight and the quality of the change improved.

If when starting to learn sequence changes the horse makes

some that are late behind, the rider must go back to working on the single changes and produce these in a more confirmed way. He must be able to position and straighten the horse as necessary before each one, and must then continue to position the horse immediately after each change, so that he can build up to making them correctly every five strides and then every four.

Drawing Back from the Rein

if the horse draws back from rein when making the tempi changes, he must be ridden well forward before starting the changes and then again on completion. The exercise of making one single flying change from a medium canter across the diagonal will help to encourage the horse forward when making a sequence of changes. When a horse draws back from the rein, it is usually because he is shy of taking the rider's hand forward. The problem could be caused by the rider's hand being 'unallowing', added to which the steps will not come through properly from behind, which usually results in the horse being croup high and then down on the shoulder. The horse must be kept well in front of the rider's leg before starting to make any of the sequence changes.

Teaching One-Time (Tempi) Changes

The one-time (tempi) changes are most difficult to accomplish and should not be tried until the horse is well balanced and confident when making the easier sequences of flying changes. When a rider who has not ridden one-time changes before reaches this standard with the first horse he has trained, and the horse must also learn this movement, the rider must get the feel of giving the aids on a schoolmaster who will respond willingly. An experienced trainer who is accomplished at teaching horses changes should train the horse up to the stage where he understands what is wanted and can make a few one-time changes easily, before the two are reunited for this exercise.

Initially, when teaching the horse or the rider one-time changes, it is best to start by asking for two changes at the end of the long side of the arena just before the corner, changing to the outside and back to the inside lead again. When the horse can do this easily from either lead, then two one-time changes must be asked for and given readily on any straight line, gradually asking for them more frequently and with fewer strides of canter between the changes.

OPPOSITE: *A horse making a tempi change from left to right.*

88

When the horse can change from inside to outside and back to inside on every third or fourth stride of canter, then three one-time changes can be attempted starting from counter canter, so that the sequence is change to the inside, then outside, and then an easy change back to the inside as the last one – if the third change were to be to the outside of the arena the horse would not find it so easy to respond.

Once three changes in a row have been accomplished from left or right canter, it is not a problem to build up to more. Athletic horses do not find this movement difficult once they have understood what is wanted. The changes are counted each time a foreleg comes to the ground. An inexperienced rider must get into the habit of counting one-time changes whenever asking for them, so that he is ready for riding an Advanced test where a set number of changes must be shown.

When giving aids for a number of changes, the first two leg aids given by the rider are made in a slightly quicker rhythm than the actual cantering strides to make it clear to the horse what is required. When the horse has picked up the one-time sequence, the aids are then given in the exact rhythm of the horse's canter. The less the rider's legs swing, the more impressive the movement appears. However, when teaching the horse the leg aids must be clear and precise, although it is not desirable to give the impression of the rider's legs being like 'windscreen wipers'. Any temptation to give a hefty rein aid should be avoided, as this would end up with the horse rocking his head from side to side.

The one-time changes should be straight, with big, springy steps that come well off the ground both in front and behind, keeping a constant speed and rhythm to stay in balance and maintain a light and even feeling on the horse's mouth. When practising these changes they must all be done on both reins so that the horse is fluent in any sequence from the right or left lead. In the official international Advanced tests the horse makes sequence changes on the diagonal or the centre line. When these are correct the horse can be asked to make the sequence changes on circles and in a variety of patterns and tempos for the Freestyle to Music test, which if done well can look extremely artistic and impressive.

OPPOSITE: *One-time changes across the diagonal – in harmony with the rider, straight and attentive.*

CHAPTER 5

PIROUETTES

A pirouette is a very difficult movement in which the horse has to describe two concentric circles, one with the hind feet and the second with the front feet. When riding a pirouette, you can either turn the horse part way or a full 360 degrees, but to be correct it must be done without losing the sequence of steps that make up the gait in which he is turning. The size of the circle made by the hind feet governs the size of the whole pirouette, a suitable size for training being up to 2m across, whereas for perfection in a Grand Prix test the inside hind leg performs its function within the three-beat canter without deviating very much from the spot. The horse's front feet and shoulders move around this axis without any loss of rhythm of the footfalls nor deviation from the pirouette size.

Advantages and Aims of the Pirouette

The pirouette is an exercise that tests the horse's reaction to the aids and the rider's ability to balance the horse and maintain the considerable control required to perform this movement. The preparatory work and the use of the pirouette in the training programme helps considerably towards developing collection. It can only be executed to a high standard when the horse is fully collected, as ultimately the horse should be able to perform a circle within the length of his body by moving the forehand round the hindquarters, whilst maintaining a uniform bend around the rider's inside leg in the direction in which he is moving.

The first pirouettes are taught whilst developing the collected walk during the Medium level work, but as the training becomes more advanced they are asked for in

collected canter. At Grand Prix level both walk and canter pirouettes have to be shown. The piaffe is the easiest gait from which to make a pirouette, as the horse is already highly collected with the footfalls in two-time, short and symmetric. This movement is not shown in the set tests, but riders like to perform it in their Freestyle to Music programme.

In competition, a half-pirouette in walk on either rein is usually required from Medium level up to Grand Prix. The half-pirouette in canter is required at Prix St George standard, and from Intermediare I and above full pirouettes

This horse is in a perfect position during a pirouette to the right. He is bent around the rider's inside leg, looking relaxed, supple and attentive.

are performed. Competitors in the Grand Prix Freestyle to Music will often perform a full walk pirouette leading into a canter pirouette, sometimes riding two or three without a break. The horse has to be extremely strong and well balanced to perform this type of movement impressively – performed badly it appears to be detrimental to the horse's capability and confidence.

Aids for the Pirouette

The aids for a pirouette are the same in any gait. Having first collected and positioned the horse around the rider's inside leg with correct bend and flexion, the inside rein brings the horse round to the direction in which the forehand is

This horse shows a good bend in a walk pirouette to the left. Note the engagement of the near hind leg.

moving, while the outside rein prevents too much bend in the neck and stops the outside shoulder from escaping to the outside. The inside leg maintains the impulsion and keeps the horse stepping forward and under his body, while the outside leg controls the hindquarters by preventing them from swinging out. The rider's weight should always be well to the inside with the body upright and still. Any inclination to step backwards while performing the pirouette is a serious fault and therefore when first asking for the movement it is best to make it large and forward so that the horse stays in front of the rider's leg, keeping a correct rhythm of the gait, and never learns to move backwards or throw himself sideways due to loss of balance through being made to perform too small a pirouette, too early on in the training.

This horse is making a very small pirouette but has come a little above the bit.

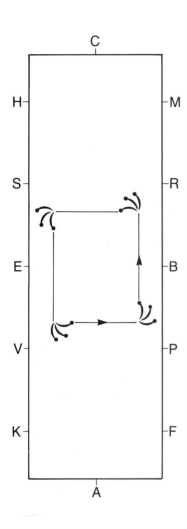

Cantering on a square, making a short 90 degree turn at the corners.

Preparation and Build-up Exercises

I favour the preparatory exercise of riding a square or rectangle and making a quarter-pirouette on each corner, which entails making two steps to the inside before riding the horse forward again on a straight line.

When first teaching the young horse the pirouette in walk or canter, this exercise has the advantage of presenting the turns in a repetitive but simple way; the distance between them can be varied to whatever the rider feels is suitable. The preparation between each corner can also be varied according to the difficulty experienced in each turn.

For example, if the hindquarters have swung to the outside, the following straight lines should be ridden in travers. If the neck has been tight and the turn lacking in bend, the line can be ridden with the neck well to the inside, followed by shoulder-in to develop more bend around the inside leg. This position will also help if the shoulders have been slow to move over or the hindquarters have stepped too much to the inside.

It is an error on the rider's part if too much outside leg is used when starting to make a pirouette, as the horse will then obey as he would when making half-pass and the inside hind leg will make steps to the inside rather than coming underneath the horse, taking more weight and ultimately being picked up and put down on the same spot.

It need not be presumed that the quarters will always swing out; in some cases the outside leg can be more effective, and useful, if used more forward on the girth to help bring the shoulders round.

Whatever the size of pirouette being attempted, the horse must stay round and supple, with a degree of bend around the rider's inside leg. The rhythm of the gait must remain consistent, and there must be sufficient impulsion and balance to enable the horse to carry out what is asked of him without his stride becoming slower or faster.

The degree of perfection obtained when riding pirouettes is an ongoing process that is connected with the development of collection. Having mastered the correct technique in walk earlier on in the training (whereby the forehand steps round the haunches while the hind legs keep the sequence of the stride in as small an area as possible), the time taken to achieve this in canter can vary enormously with each horse.

This working trot, shown on a straight line and then correctly following the line of a circle, is very difficult to fault.

ABOVE: *A well-balanced collected trot, with the hocks well engaged and the shoulders and neck correctly raised and arched.*

LEFT AND RIGHT: *This horse is showing the balance and lightness of the forehand that marks collected canter, and the correct bend around the rider's inside leg while making a small circle.*

LEFT: *A classically correct piaffe, with the hindquarters slightly lowered and forehand light and free to make the elevated steps.*

RIGHT: *Teaching piaffe while mounted. This shows how the horse makes short trot steps from collected walk.*

BELOW: *Teaching piaffe in hand, with side reins, lunge cavesson and rein.*

Teaching piaffe and passage while working the horse in long reins.

ABOVE: *Loosening up the horse on a small circle.*

RIGHT: *Some shortened steps in trot: half-collection.*

OPPOSITE TOP: *Keeping the horse extra round, to encourage the use of his back while making the first piaffe steps.*

OPPOSITE BOTTOM: *Starting some piaffe steps while moving forward. An athletic horse may offer passage from this exercise.*

TOP: *Horses in freedom often demonstrate that the paces asked for in dressage training are not unnatural. Here an Alter-Real stallion bred in Portugal shows extended trot across his paddock.*

CENTRE: *The same stallion making passage steps, with an unusual bend in his neck to look at the camera.*

BOTTOM: *A Saddlebred horse showing elevated steps. These American horses were not bred for competition dressage and, indeed, have many unusual specialities in addition to the normal walk, trot and canter required by the FEI. Nevertheless, this photograph shows that piaffe-type steps are not unnatural to a horse.*

Developing the Pirouette Canter

Firstly, the horse has to develop what I call the 'pirouette canter'. This can take a year or more from the Medium level and should not be hurried, but built up progressively, allowing the muscles in the horse's haunches to strengthen. The muscles on the young horse's forearms are stronger and harder to the touch than those in a similar position between the hock and stifle on the hind leg. During training this will even up, as the muscles in the back and hindquarters strengthen and carry more weight. Pirouettes in canter should not be attempted until the horse has reached the physical maturity to carry out the exercise easily, without incurring aching muscles and therefore a dislike of the movement.

There are various exercises that help to develop this 'pirouette canter'. The aim is to be able to make a transition from a good forward-going canter back to a shorter outline, with obvious shorter steps and the speed of the canter comparable with that of the horse's walk. To achieve this, the hind legs must step well under the horse's body, with the haunches lowering and the angle of the joints increasing as a greater part of the body weight is transferred on to them. This position can incur a great deal of strain, so only a few short steps should be asked for at any one time, starting with as few as four or five before riding more forward again. The acceptance of the rein with a soft contact should be maintained throughout all preparatory work and during the execution of pirouettes. If the rein is too strong because the horse is being held at a slow speed or forced to turn on a short radius, his back will 'lock up' and the steps will lose their quality, as it is too difficult for a horse to take short and springy steps in this way.

An Advanced Medium level horse should be quite accomplished at coming back to collection from a medium or extended canter without deviating on to two tracks or resisting in the mouth. At a more advanced level he will be required to take fewer of the intermediary-length steps between the extensions and the collected paces, with an obvious lowering of the croup as he does so. This lowering of the haunches as a result of the increased collection is the key to producing a controlled small pirouette, with three to four canter strides being taken to accomplish 180 degrees (a half-pirouette) and six to eight strides to turn the 360 degrees of a full pirouette.

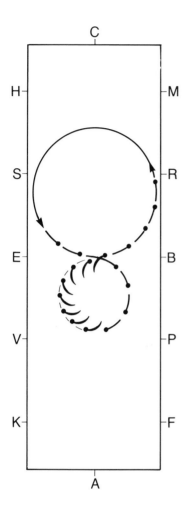

A 20m circle in counter canter leading into a volte, or a pasade if the hindquarters are placed to the inside.

The canter steps must remain small and elevated during the turn, with a regular and easily recognizable three-time beat all the way round. This is why it is necessary to establish the very slow canter with short steps on a straight line before asking the horse to make the short turns necessary to produce a pirouette. If the horse is asked to make a short turn while taking long steps he will become overbalanced and on the forehand, the long steps making the croup higher than the shoulders as he endeavours to turn without having attained the necessary collection.

Using Counter Canter, Voltes and Half-Passes

In order to develop this canter, the horse is worked in counter canter on circles to help loosen up the hindquarters. It is helpful to push the horse actively forward in counter canter on a large circle to make sure the steps are coming through from behind, before coming back to a collected canter. As the steps shorten they must come higher off the ground, due to the bending of the joints in the hind legs.

A good way of assessing the collection is to work the horse on a large circle in counter canter and then make a volte (6m circle) to the outside in true canter. If a horse cannot make a volte correctly, keeping the balance, suppleness, rhythm and speed constant, then he is not yet ready to perform pirouettes. It is a useful preparation to ride the volte frequently at any place in the arena while developing the canter. Another useful exercise is to spiral down to a volte from 20m circle and then make two or three small circles before spiralling out again. This exercise is good because the horse can easily be pushed more forward on to the larger circle if the hind steps are not coming through on the smaller circles.

Making canter half-passes at a steeper angle will also help to engage the hindquarters and increase the mobility of the horse. A good preparation for the pirouette is to ride a half-pass to the centre line from a corner, then ride straight down the centre line, near the end make a half-circle with the quarters to the inside, and then return in half-pass to the centre line. The first half-pass can finish at X and the first half-circle can be 10m, then gradually the half-pass can be performed on a more acute line to the centre and the half-circle made smaller, until the horse is performing a half-pasade – a 6m circle with the hindquarters to the inside. This exercise again allows the rider to push the horse more forward on the centre line before coming back with increased engagement at either end. It also gives the rider a chance to

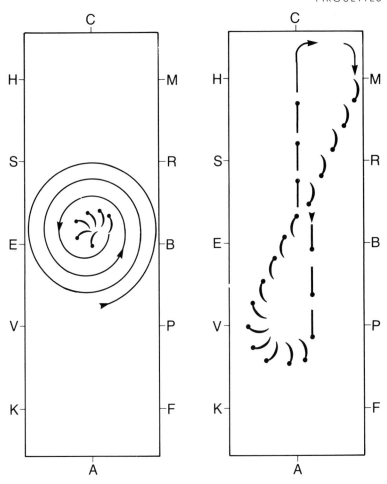

straighten the horse between the lateral work. The ability to do this is most important and should constantly be checked.

Using Renvers and Travers

I have found that working the horse in the position of renvers is one of the most useful exercises for increasing the engagement of the hindquarters. Although it is the same movement as travers, the hindquarters move along the wall or fence of the arena, which helps to keep the horse steady on a line without escaping work by falling out or losing the angle. In travers the horse's hindquarters are deliberately put to the inside of the track which, if done too often, can make it difficult to straighten the horse on the long side of the arena when riding in medium or extended canter. The renvers position will help with this problem by increasing the engagement of the inside hind leg to a remarkable degree.

LEFT: *Spiralling in from a 20m circle in canter, putting the hindquarters in when the circle reaches 8m.*

RIGHT: *Half-pass to the centre line, down the centre line and half-circle with the hindquarters in, then return in half-pass to the centre line. This exercise can be performed in trot or canter. In canter, it prepares the horse for pirouettes.*

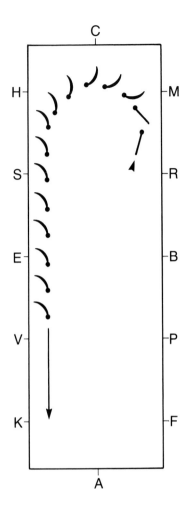

C

H — — M

S — — R

E — — B

V — — P

K — — F

A

Renvers to the outside of a large circle and continuing down the inside of the track. This exercise is very helpful for horses that are always trying to change from counter canter.

A good way of positioning the horse in renvers is to ride half-pass from the centre line to the outside track, finishing with the shoulders on the inside of the track and the hindquarters on the track, with the horse remaining bent around the rider's inside leg. Then ride on down the track and on to a counter-canter circle, before continuing in renvers along the next long side. The most difficult place to make renvers is on a circle, with the canter lead to the outside and the hindquarters making a larger circle than the forehand.

Travers on a circle can also be used to encourage more weight on to the inside hind leg. Spiralling the circle smaller in this position will eventually end up as a pasade, and still smaller will constitute a large pirouette. This is a good way of introducing the horse to the movement, but the rider must remember to stop pushing the hindquarters to the inside when the circle gets really small, and concentrate on turning the shoulders around the haunches.

These exercises are very demanding, and the amount they are used must relate to the ability and strength of the horse. They should be introduced gradually into the daily training sessions, and care must be taken not to increase the engagement of the hindquarters for too long a period. It is essential to ride the horse actively forward during the lateral work to freshen up the canter, and if the canter becomes flat or the steps cease to 'work through', the horse must be worked in a way that improves this, while the more advanced lateral work is discontinued for a while.

It is important to keep the quality of the canter at all times. If the horse has made a big effort and the rider feels that the hindquarters have been lowered and the hind legs more engaged, he should be allowed to relax in walk on a long rein and be rewarded. It is possible that the horse may resent this type of work until his muscles have developed, as he will find it difficult. However, the muscles will not develop unless the horse is asked to use them, and so it is the rider's task to establish the correct exercises in a way that improves the horse without causing discomfort and tension.

Practising Pirouettes

When the pirouette canter has been established to a satisfactory degree, the half-pirouette can be introduced. It is easier for the horse to make the pirouette from a circle, but in tests it is asked for on a straight line, which is why I like to ride a square while training. A half-pirouette is merely two corners

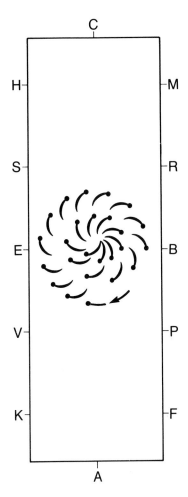

ABOVE: *Spiralling in on a circle in travers and making a large pirouette in the centre of the circle, before circling out again.*

LEFT: *A horse correctly prepared for a pirouette to the right. Note the softness in the mouth and the excellent bend in the body around the rider's right leg.*

of the square put together, and it can help to ride the first half-pirouettes with that in mind, especially if the rider is learning along with the horse. It is also a great help to ride the movement in front of a mirror, as the rider will learn to feel the problems as he sees them – it can be difficult for an inexperienced rider to assess the size of the pirouette and the steps that the horse is taking. Filming with a video and then watching the work is even better.

101

Initially, pirouettes should never be ridden too small, and even when the horse is ready to compete the size of the pirouette required for the test should not be practised endlessly at home. Problems normally occur from trying to make the pirouette too small. The judges will give a high mark to a slightly larger pirouette if the horse stays round in his outline, keeps the sequence of canter steps and the canter rhythm, and stays supple and bent around the rider's inside leg while showing an ability to lower the haunches. If the rider makes the pirouette too small before the horse is able to handle the difficulties this involves, the horse is likely to:

● Brace against the tight turn and may pivot on the inside hind leg.

● Lurch around by lifting the forehand too high.

● Lose the true three-beat sequence of canter steps by jumping the hind legs together.

● Hollow during the turn and stiffen against the rider's hand.

● Change legs on the way round or as he moves out of a pirouette.

These faults will result in the judge giving a very low mark.

The hindquarters may swing out as the weight falls on to the inside shoulder, losing the bend and therefore the ability to bring the shoulders round the hindquarters. Some horses will become very adept at cantering the smallest possible voltes with the hind steps following in the path of the front feet in a beautifully collected canter. However small this circle may be it is not a pirouette, and the rider should apply more outside leg to keep the hindquarters more in the centre of the circle while keeping his weight well to the inside to help to bring the shoulders round.

As when teaching the horse flying changes, it is most helpful to have an experienced person on the ground to help rectify any problems as they occur. Horses will experience varying degrees of difficulty, and the preparation and aids given during the pirouette must vary accordingly.

As the build-up work progresses and the rider feels the canter become good enough to start making pirouettes, it is normal to ride a pirouette at any convenient place in the arena when the right moment presents itself. Until the horse is very proficient, it is better to work on one pirouette at a time rather than chop and change about from one side to the

OPPOSITE: *This competitor is making a very small pirouette, showing a considerable bend in the horse's body. The rider's weight is well to the inside. Only the most talented horses can maintain a whole pirouette in this position.*

1

2

The sequence of photographs on these two pages shows all the requirements of a well-executed pirouette to the left. The horse remains softly on the bit, keeping the bend, impulsion and balance, and maintaining the correct canter sequence of footfalls whilst turning within his own body length. The hindquarters are well engaged and lowered, showing a perfect flexion of all the joints.

other. Having worked on the canter and used some of the exercises already described, make a few pasades and short turns on some of the corners to check that the horse is on the aids, the most important factor being that the horse will move forward from the inside leg before, during, or after making a pirouette. A lot of the other problems mentioned will be alleviated if this one point is kept in mind. It is vital to be able to ride a horse actively forward out of a half- or a whole pirouette, and if some problems have occurred during the movement the best thing is to ride out of the pirouette and then start again. Young horses must not be allowed to anticipate and start the pirouette without being asked, so always ride forward again if you feel this is happening.

3

4

5

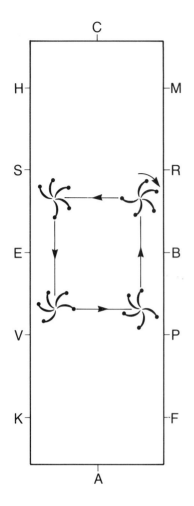

Having made a few easy, large pirouettes without the horse becoming tense, they can then be attempted at more difficult points in the arena. Asking for a pirouette from a larger counter-canter circle is a helpful way of preventing a horse from anticipating, because the turn to the outside of the circle is not so obvious to the horse. However, the counter canter must be collected enough to make such a turn.

A more difficult place to ask for the movement is from counter canter on the inside of the track, so that the pirouette can be executed by turning towards the boards or fence. This is useful if the horse is inclined to gain too much ground forwards during the turn, as the wall prevents this and encourages the horse to come round.

An exercise favoured at the Spanish Riding School in Vienna is to ride a square in counter canter away from the track, leaving enough room to perform three-quarters of a pirouette to the outside in each corner of the square. This is a great test of concentration and control, and an excellent step between the half-pirouette and the whole pirouette.

Having achieved some pirouettes to one side that are well up to standard, the horse should be rewarded and given a walk on a long rein before doing the same to the other side. Different problems will be evident on each rein, and the preparation and corrections should be varied accordingly.

Prix St George

At Prix St George level the half-pirouettes are asked for on a straight line on the first half of a diagonal, or on the centre line having first described a half-circle or serpentine loop, the latter being the easiest to perform as the line of the serpentine helps to develop the canter around the rider's inside leg. However, in the last three strides of canter before making the turn the horse must be placed in a slight shoulder-in position on a straight line, otherwise more than half a pirouette will have to be executed before you can come out and continue the serpentine. The turn should not be started until the front feet have crossed the centre line, thus allowing the steps of the hind feet to be made on the line and giving plenty of room to come out of the pirouette and make the following loop back if desired. It is easier at first to come out of a half-pirouette on a curved line, but ultimately both horse and rider must be proficient at keeping on a straight line before and after the pirouettes.

Pirouettes on the diagonal line can present you with the

Counter canter on a square, making three-quarters of a pirouette in each corner. The square must be on the inside of the track to leave room to make the corners to the outside. This movement originated at the Spanish Riding School in Vienna.

problem of getting the young horse sufficiently collected. This is because the horse associates the diagonal line with extensions and flying changes that are ridden more forward, and therefore may be disinclined to slow down and shorten the outline. The rider must use the corner before the diagonal to make a half-halt to ensure that the horse is balanced and collected. A slight shoulder-fore position should be maintained from the quarter marker up to the point of making the pirouette before the X marker. At this stage it is a mistake to ask the young horse just coming up to this standard of work for too much bend, as it adds to the difficulty of the movement. It is far more important to maintain the sequence of the canter and the balance – more bend can be acquired as suppleness and confidence are established.

When riding the half-pirouette it helps to concentrate first on keeping the canter steps on a straight line in shoulder-fore position, then to make two very positive steps of the pirouette, concentrating on getting the shoulders to turn precisely to the inside. The next two steps usually need more help from the rider's outside leg as the quarters are more likely to escape in the second half of the pirouette. The rider's inside leg keeps the horse moving forward and prevents the shoulders from lurching to the inside of the turn. The first two steps are usually managed in a correct manner if the rider's weight stays to the inside and the rein does not become restrictive.

Finally, look at the quarter marker you came from and ride positively back down the same line. This is a useful way of thinking what to do whilst learning to ride this movement and is a good technique to perfect. It is important not to get stuck in the 'pirouette canter' once the turn has been completed, but ride more forward so that a good fluent change can be made at the marker, and not before.

When making whole pirouettes the horse has to be sufficiently developed both physically and mentally to keep the balance and short steps for twice the length of time needed for half-pirouettes. Again, the pirouettes must gradually be made smaller as the horse becomes more proficient. They should not be over-practised because of the strain they put on the horse's muscles.

The distance between whole pirouettes required in the Intermediare I standard test and upwards varies. It is still important to ride actively forwards out of the pirouette into the flying change, but after the change the horse must be shortened and collected as quickly as possible so that he is

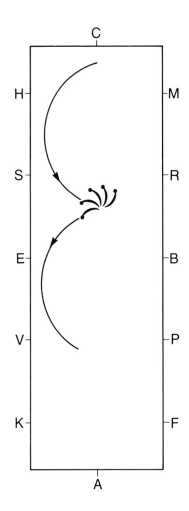

A serpentine loop into a half-pirouette. This is a good place to make a half-pirouette, as the horse can be shortened and prepared on the half-circle.

This horse has overbalanced into a pirouette left off the centre line, becoming croup high with the weight down on the left shoulder.

balanced sufficiently for the second pirouette.

Pirouettes are nearly always ridden after a turn on to the diagonal or a turn on to the centre line. Both these turns can be used as a preparation for the pirouette itself, as they will help to get the horse balanced and around and in front of the rider's inside leg.

Grand Prix

When the horse has reached Grand Prix level much of the work is required on the centre line, including the pirouettes. It is therefore necessary from an early stage to spend a lot of time training on the centre line, not only to perfect the entry into the halt from trot and canter, but also the rein back and the various transitions involved, including piaffe, passage and the flying changes.

If a horse canters down the centre line with the near fore leading and performs a good pirouette to the left at some point on that line, the hind legs should move marginally forward, keeping the three-time sequence of steps, with the inside hind leg, if perfect, describing a circle no larger than a

ABOVE: *The rider has corrected the position and balance on the way round.*

LEFT: *Completing the pirouette in a better shape, although it is finishing some way off the centre line.*

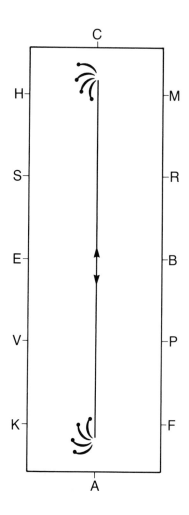

Half-pirouette in walk or canter alternately at each end of the centre line. The horse can be asked to canter half-way round a walk pirouette.

soup plate placed to the left of the line with one edge touching it. In this way the horse can finish the pirouette and move forward totally straight on the line, and vice versa when turning the opposite way.

Pirouettes in Walk

It is useful to work up and down the centre line making half-pirouettes at either end, starting in walk and then progressing to canter, and making a full pirouette on the line when desired. If the horse is slow to bring the shoulders round in canter, he can be reminded of what is wanted in walk and then asked to canter during the walk pirouette or as he comes out of it. A full walk pirouette is a useful preparation for canter pirouettes, as there is less tension and strain on the muscles. If the horse gets strong in the rein in canter, I like to go back to walk and make these pirouettes with the rein lighter. By doing this it is often possible to discover why the rein becomes strong and make the necessary corrections.

The walk pirouette also helps to develop the collected walk, especially with a horse that has a big stride and overtracks considerably, when it is a problem for the rider to shorten these steps without spoiling the correct rhythm. When the rein is taken a little more strongly to encourage the horse to walk at a slower speed, the usual result is that the horse slows down the rhythm and develops a lateral walk. If the horse is asked to make a walk pirouette without the rein getting strong, the result of a short step being lifted higher from the ground can be reflected in the collection of the walk. Thus, making two or three steps of walk pirouette at various intervals while working on the collected walk can help to develop this movement in the correct way.

In a similar way, the walk pirouette can help to improve the collected trot. A transition from trot to walk, followed immediately by a half or whole walk pirouette and then immediately back into collected trot, will engage the hind legs and encourage them to step further the body weight. In both these instances, the walk pirouettes should be made large enough to keep the horse thinking forward and the steps active. A pirouette that is lazy will not improve the following gait, and with this in mind the larger-sized pirouettes both in walk and canter should be used most frequently during training and the smaller ones required in competition will improve as a result.

The walk pirouettes are a lot easier to perform than those

These pictures show a horse completing a pirouette to the right and continuing in collected canter with quarters still lowered and well engaged.

in canter, but the care and training put into them will be reflected in the more difficult movement, which I consider to be the most testing requirement of the advanced tests. Only years of training many different horses will produce a skilled rider who can show them in effortless style.

CHAPTER 6

PIAFFE AND
WORK IN HAND

The piaffe is the ultimate in collection, as the horse contains his impulsion, performing trot with little or no forward movement but keeping all the qualities of the collected trot. As in the canter pirouettes, the horse's hindquarters should be slightly lowered and the hind legs more actively engaged, so that they take more weight. This will result in the forehand being lightened, so that the front feet are raised higher than the back feet as they are elevated in diagonal pairs. To be more precise, the horse's front foot should be level with the centre of the opposite cannon bone, with the forearm being almost horizontal. The back foot is lifted only just above the fetlock joint of the opposite hind leg when it is on the ground. There is an extremely springy and cadenced rhythm within these elevated steps, with a very short moment of suspension.

Piaffe or Passage First?

Horses will often show some aptitude for piaffe or passage during their early training – usually when they are excited or become upset. Some trainers will start with whichever movement the horse appears naturally to find the easiest. However, it is generally thought that the piaffe should be taught first, because if the passage is well confirmed it can be difficult to teach the horse to make the elevated steps required for piaffe, without the horse offering the forward suspension wanted in the passage.

Again, there are different views on how to obtain those often elusive first steps of piaffe. Some trainers gain them by creating tension within the collected trot, but I personally prefer to explain to the horse what is wanted while keeping him obedient, supple and relaxed, as this will in the long term result in a more energetic and rhythmic piaffe. The horse does not require a great deal of impulsion when first making a few steps of piaffe; in fact, a lot of impulsion can be a hindrance, as the horse will not know how to handle the impulsion without being able to move forward, and this often results in the hind steps becoming too high and the croup being raised from too much activity.

A correct piaffe.

*An unusual photograph,
showing clearly the correct lift
of the feet in piaffe.*

Preparation for Piaffe

The first difficulty to overcome is teaching the horse to take the smallest possible trot steps in a relaxed manner. This can be done when the horse is either being ridden or worked in hand. Some horses can get extremely strong and boisterous in hand, especially if they do not initially understand what is wanted. If they are not owned or trained by a person who is strong enough to control them or sufficiently knowledgeable in the technique, it is not a good method to use.

A Prix St George horse just starting piaffe, making correct steps with very little impulsion. A horse learning piaffe should not lower the haunches any more than this.

During the preparation for piaffe time is well spent riding the horse in 'half-collection' in trot. This can be compared to the irritating 'jogging' that horses often make when they are too excited or too tense to walk properly. The horse should be worked on the track round the arena, as the wall or fence will help to prevent the hindquarters swinging. During all preparatory work for piaffe, the horse must be kept straight. Making transitions from walk into a slow, creeping-forward trot for a few steps and then back to walk for a few steps, with each gait being of five to ten steps, is a good way of getting the horse to lower and engage his hindquarters. However, the trot must be made with the rein soft, not holding the horse slow.

At the beginning the horse will probably not understand what is wanted and may have to be touched with the stick to be made to go forward in trot, having been frequently brought back to walk in the past when the trot had become too fast. If he is patted and praised when achieving the right steps at the right speed, he will soon get the idea of what is wanted. It can take weeks rather than days before the horse gets really proficient at taking the short steps. However, these are the foundation for putting the spring, elevation and bounce into the trot steps to create piaffe, with the horse realizing he does not have to make too much ground forward in order to do so.

This slow trot should not be produced because the horse does not want to go forward and has dropped behind the rein contact. The horse must remain round, working through the rein and accepting the forward driving aids and the slowing down aids with increased obedience. As soon as he has accomplished the short steps, the horse has to learn to make them with increased activity and height.

The Aids — Leg, Voice and Stick

It is during this time that I like to introduce the voice by clicking with the tongue as the horse goes into the half-speed trot. If the horse does not react to this voice aid he is touched with the stick. The voice can be used in an urgent manner or in a rhythm with the trot, and later on it will be associated with making the piaffe steps.

If at any time during this work or at other moments during the training the horse offers a piaffe step, he must be rewarded immediately. My aids for piaffe are to use the legs together in the trot rhythm on the girth and, depending on the horse's sensitivity, these can be made with a very slight nudge from an already secure leg contact or by gentle use of the spur. During the work in this half-collected trot the aids for piaffe are not used, but the aids used for going into trot along with half-halts, use of the voice and transitions to walk, are all refined. It is a great advantage if piaffe can be taught without too much use of the stick, as the stick is not allowed in international competition and therefore the horse must be trained to be obedient to the leg to perform this movement. A clever horse will soon realize that the stick is not used in competition and so the rider cannot afford to depend on it to produce the piaffe. I believe tension should be avoided if possible; however, a laid back or less sensitive horse may initially have to be made tense in order to achieve the desired result.

Work in Hand

The advantage of teaching horses piaffe in hand is that without the weight of the rider on his back, the horse will find it easier to 'bounce' on the spot and learn the movement. The main disadvantage is that the horse does not learn to work through the rein properly when the piaffe is first intro-

This photograph shows the correct equipment for working in hand and the horse making some small piaffe steps.

duced, which can result in the front steps not coming off the ground sufficiently.

The equipment used to work the horse is hand is the same as that used for lungeing except for the lunge line, which can be replaced with a shorter lead rope or a headcollar rope. The lunge whip can be replaced by a long, firm stick that can easily reach the horse's haunches when the trainer is standing by the shoulders. Having first loosened the horse by lungeing him in the normal manner, he is made to stand on the track against the wall while the side reins are shortened, so that he stays round and in a collected outline. The side reins should be adjusted to a length that allows the horse's head and neck to be raised and rounded with the nose just in front of the vertical. If they are too short, he may well lock up in his neck and back and will not be able to make the correct steps, and will also be very uncomfortable.

The trainer stands with his back to the direction of movement and the line from the front of the cavesson in his left hand held at a comfortable height half-way up the horse's neck. With the stick in his right hand, he walks backwards, remaining alongside the horse's front legs. The whip should be used to stroke the horse on the neck, flank and haunches as well as to touch the legs, so that the horse is not anxious when the trainer is carrying a long whip. He can then encourage the horse to make a few short steps forward in trot by using the voice and, if necessary, a tap with the stick on the haunches. The horse should never be made afraid of the stick and the aim should be to give the lightest aid possible to gain the reaction needed. At this stage the trainer should not try to achieve an elevated step: the aim is that the horse should creep forward at walk speed taking relaxed, small but correct trot steps with a supple back and confident manner, as described when under saddle. Frequent transitions from halt to trot are made, and as the horse shortens himself by bringing the hind legs underneath the body the side reins can be shortened accordingly.

It is possible to work the horse in hand with two people, one standing by the head and controlling the horse with the cavesson while the other walks by the saddle, holding the whip and helping to keep the horse straight whilst encouraging the correct steps. It is unwise to walk with the side reins too short for fear of spoiling the walk steps. In hand, the horse needs to be allowed to stretch the neck with the possibility of more movement to keep an acceptable walk.

It is also possible to work the horse in hand by holding

both reins of the bridle in the left hand over the horse's neck in front of the withers, as an alternative to using a cavesson and side reins. The trainer should be tall enough to keep a reasonable contact and to control the horse in this position.

When the horse has accepted this discipline and offers the type of trot required (comparable to the extra-slow pirouette canter but without so much impulsion), then the trainer can encourage him to put spring and elevation into these little steps by using the stick at a place that causes the desired reaction, usually on the haunches or below the hock, as the horse is moving very slightly forward. If during this shortening of the trot the horse appears to keep the front legs very straight, a slight tap with the stick will encourage him to lift the leg with a bending of the knee.

I do not recommend excessive use of the stick on either the front or back legs as it can produce tense, earthbound steps

Working in hand with a cavesson and side reins, touching the horse gently on the foreleg to encourage lift with a bend in the knee.

that do not encourage the horse to spring from one diagonal to another, and will often result in a horse that will only piaffe if somebody is on the ground with a stick, instead of obeying the rider's leg aids. If the stick is used too severely at the top of the haunches it will cause the horse to lift the quarters too high as he makes a springy step – the opposite of what is required, as the croup should be lowered and the hind legs carry an increased amount of weight as the forehand is raised and lightened. One must guard against the horse learning to lift the quarters, making piaffe-type steps with the hind legs whilst only stepping forwards with the front legs.

As soon as the horse offers any sort of spring or bounce into the step he must be halted immediately and rewarded. It may take weeks to prepare the horse for this type of work, but with care and patience a successful piaffe can be produced with the horse moving minimally forward, with each step being one footfall in front of the next. A light rider can then be put on the horse, so that he can get used to making the same steps with a weight on his back and be introduced gradually to the piaffe aids from the rider, with the trainer on the ground doing less and less.

When the horse has understood what is required and is making a few piaffe steps to the aids given by the rider's legs (and voice when necessary), the most difficult part of the training is over. The rider must now improve the quality and number of steps and add impulsion to the movement. I find that putting too much impulsion into the steps too quickly can produce unlevel steps, loss of rhythm and a non-acceptance of the rein, all of which are required to earn high marks for this movement.

The old classical masters were renowned for making piaffe between the pillars, and this method is still used today by the Spanish Riding School in Vienna and the Cadre Noir in Saumur. However, with the Thoroughbred type of horse that is more favoured at present, and the rules that are laid down by the FEI as to what is required, the more relaxed and forward method of working in hand is probably more suitable for today's competition requirements. The Thoroughbred type of horse does not have the equable temperament required for the discipline of work between the pillars, and may develop problems that are very difficult to cure when under saddle, the most likely being tension that will cause unlevel steps, loss of rhythm and too much elevation in the hind steps, creating a croup-high outline or possibly even a total lack of co-operation.

Work in Long Reins

Another method of working the horse in hand is with long reins. Because these are fitted through rings on a roller or a loop in front of the saddle, the horse can be brought back to a shorter outline for the half-collected or piaffe steps and then allowed to stretch the topline and trot more forward in a circle round the trainer. In this way the work can be more varied when long reining. It is also easier to keep the horse working more forward with this method; however, the trainer must be experienced at holding the reins and handling the stick before attempting the advanced work.

Working forward with long reins.

The development of the piaffe must proceed with much patience and tact. It is very unwise to hurry or force any improvement, especially if the horse is young and not yet developed physically to full strength. The steps should always gain a little ground forward until such time as the horse is in perfect balance, working through the rein and showing some ability to lower the haunches. Thoroughbred horses often have difficulty in achieving this due to their longer and weaker hind legs; warmblood horses usually have more powerful hindquarters. Whatever the shape of the horse, it is a great strain to lower the croup, and plenty of time must be allowed for each horse to strengthen the necessary muscles.

Transitions from halt and walk into piaffe and back again will help to bring the hindquarters under the horse and accustom him to making the more difficult transitions required later from passage to piaffe and back into passage. The piaffe steps should not be practised for too long at a time – it is better to work two or three times on the piaffe during a training session, and if a horse has made a few steps really well, reward him by trotting forward. The piaffe will help to

This photograph shows how the reins are attached at the top of the saddle to allow the horse forward with a longer neck if necessary.

improve the collected work in canter as well as trot, due to the more advanced balance and engagement.

Difficulties and Corrections

A horse learning to piaffe on long reins. Here the reins are attached to the girth and ensure that the horse stays round enough for this exercise.

The problems that occur in piaffe are mainly due to physical difficulties on the horse's part, or training and rider errors which result in a failure to lift the horse's forelegs high enough. This is often the case with a Thoroughbred horse that naturally has a very flat action in the trot – horses with a rounded action of the front steps find it easier to piaffe.

As well as being a physical problem, this is also a symptom

This horse is showing technically correct steps with both front and hind feet.

of the horse not working through the rein correctly, usually resulting in him leaning on the rider's hand. When this has been improved and the horse has learnt to 'sit' more behind, the shoulders will lighten and the horse's knees can be raised higher. This lack of lift in the front legs is often seen in conjunction with a high croup and the horse trying to piaffe without bending the hind legs. There is a lack of suppleness in the back and the horse is usually lowering the shoulders and not working into the rider's hand with correct rein contact. In these circumstances the horse must be worked quietly forward a few steps at a time, with many transitions

to improve the rein contact and the engagement. Making piaffe on the spot should not be attempted until these aspects have been improved.

The inability to remain in balance will show itself in several ways. The horse may rock from side to side so that there is always one front foot on the ground, and this is often accompanied by the horse crossing over his legs, either in front or behind, and is usually a symptom of insufficient bending of the hocks. If the horse is markedly stiff to one side, through tension or unevenness in the rein, one hind leg will be lifted higher than the other. All these problems must

The front leg is rather straight – a problem with the more Thoroughbred type of horse when performing piaffe.

be improved by working the horse forward in a very relaxed and low-key manner, just as when first teaching the movement. A horse that physically finds the movement difficult must be given a great deal of time to overcome his individual problems, otherwise many unwanted faults will manifest themselves needlessly.

If the front legs get stuck in one place and the hind legs creep forward too much under the body (rather like the position of an elephant standing on a drum at the circus), the activation must be stopped and the horse should be moved forwards and started again, as it is impossible for him to make piaffe steps in this position for too long, and even more difficult for him to move forward into passage. Care must be taken to keep the steps moving forward initially, so that this position does not materialize through over collection and the horse getting 'stuck on the spot'.

Some horses will benefit from the trainer encouraging and backing up the rider's aids with discreet used of the whip from the ground. Others will not accept this approach and the resulting tension will make the piaffe steps worse rather than better. All horses vary as to the amount of work and pressure they can take when learning this movement and it is up to the rider to discover the best way to teach the piaffe and

Here the knee is being lifted correctly.

improve the quality of the steps. On no account must the horse be made agitated and discover how to quicken and hurry the rhythm, which will result in little or no elevation, as this is a very difficult problem to cure.

A horse that seems totally unable to understand what is wanted in the school, can sometimes be made to understand whilst out on a hack. The rider can produce a few steps, reward the horse and progress from there on. Asking for piaffe when riding out will often improve the quality of the

This horse is showing good steps but is a little low in the shoulder, with the nose behind the vertical.

Here the front legs have not moved forward sufficiently and the hind legs are too far under the body, making the horse a little tense. He should be patted and allowed to relax, having made a few steps in this difficult position.

steps and the gaiety of the movement, especially if you ride behind another horse and allow it to go on ahead. However, care should be taken that this does not cause the horse to start leaping into the air to catch up with his companion. This would only make the horse ill-mannered and difficult to ride out.

Asking for piaffe whilst riding down a slight slope will greatly increase the engagement and the lowering of the hindquarters, so it is helpful to find a slope that can be used regularly in this way to get the horse used to bringing his hind legs further underneath his body.

As the piaffe improves more steps can be asked for, and the horse must then be asked to perform the movement away

An Oldenburg stallion demonstrating that natural elevation in trot and canter comes easily to horses when loose in a paddock.

The Arab horse is accepted as the purest of breeds, renowned for its endurance and ability to carry heavy riders over a long distance. It does not come naturally to these horses to produce the rounded outline or weight-carrying engagement of the hind legs needed for dressage. However, when crossed with other breeds their characteristic beauty, elegance and strength have produced good competition horses. These two pictures show the type of elevation that could be the beginnings of passage when training a dressage horse.

LEFT: *Carl Hester was the highest placed British competitor at the 1992 Olympic Games in Barcelona. He is seen here on Giorgione, riding a half-pass to the left.*

BELOW: *Nicole Uphoff riding Rembrandt at the 1992 Olympics, showing impressive spring and engagement in canter. Rembrandt won the Individual Gold Medal, as well as a Team Gold Medal for Germany.*

OPPOSITE: *Klaus Balkenhol at the 1992 Olympics riding Goldstern, on whom he won the Individual Bronze Medal and Team Gold for Germany. Here Goldstern is showing large, impressive one-time changes.*

ABOVE: *Monica Theodorescu of Germany on Grunox, showing a classical piaffe.*

LEFT: *Monica Theodorescu showing a pirouette left, with Grunox perfectly balanced and bent around her inside leg.*

Kyra Kyrkland of Finland riding Matador in a perfect piaffe (left) and extended trot (above) at the 1988 Olympic Games in Seoul, where she came fifth in the individual competition. They went on to win the Silver Medal at the first World Equestrian Games in Sweden in 1990.

ABOVE: *The author riding Wily Imp in extended trot at the 1988 Olympics.*

LEFT: *Wily Imp: the final halt and salute at the end of the test.*

ABOVE: *A powerful passage: Otto Hofer of Switzerland riding Andiamo at the 1988 Olympics.*

RIGHT: *Christine Stuckelberger of Switzerland riding Gaugin de Lully, showing the impressive half-pass steps for which she is renowned. She was Individual Bronze Medal winner at the 1988 Olympics.*

from the track. Without the stabilizing influence of the wall the horse may become crooked, due to his weight falling on to one shoulder. In this case the horse must accept the discipline of going into piaffe from a shoulder-fore position and be worked more forward off the track until the balance has improved.

Piaffe down a slope to engage the hindquarters and counteract a lifting of the croup.

The temperament of each individual horse probably has more influence on the piaffe than on any other movement. Horses with a high-spirited and sensitive character have to be handled with great care, as too much prressure or the inability to correct disobedience with confidence and quiet control on the part of the trainer can prolong the length of time before any result is achieved. If handled correctly, horses with this temperament will often produce a more exciting and impressive piaffe in the long run.

The horse whose character is steadier and more laid back may be more difficult to encourage to spring off the ground and remain on the spot. Care must be taken that too much stick is not used to achieve this, as the horse can go sour and in the long run will not produce piaffe from the leg aids at all. To this end, care must be taken during the earlier training that the horse remains obedient to the leg aids without having to use excessive whip or spur.

Influence of the Leg Aids

The leg aids can be used to influence the rhythm of the piaffe – if the steps are too slow, the rider's legs can be applied with an increased tempo. The position of the legs to give the aids will vary from person to person, but the horse will pick up the piaffe aid if it is consistently used. As the piaffe becomes more confirmed and extra spring is asked for, the position of the leg aids may influence either the front or the hind legs of the horse and should be used accordingly.

Some riders use diagonal aids in conjunction with the diagonal steps of the horse. This may have the desired result of increasing the height of the diagonal step, or it may cause the horse to start swinging or rocking the quarters. One fact is certain, whatever aid is used for piaffe it must be different and easily distinguishable from that used for passage, as a great many transitions into and out of these gaits have to be performed when competing at Grand Prix level.

The Outline

The outline of the horse can have a great influence on the quality of the piaffe steps. If the shoulders stay down and the head and neck come higher, the horse's back will dip and the hind legs will go too far out behind. The result of this will be

Working the horse in piaffe in a 'deep' outline.

that the horse appears to be in two parts. In this position the muscles along the bottom of the neck are usually used to support the forehand, and the horse will not be working through the rein in the desired manner. If this happens, the horse must be worked forward and rounded in his outline, before being asked for piaffe again with the hindlegs more underneath him.

Piaffe with the horse not lowering the croup, the neck too short and the nose behind the vertical.

131

To strengthen the back and encourage more engagement from behind, it can help to work the horse in an extra-deep outline, to let the shoulders come up rather than just the neck. If the rider can release the rein for a few steps of piaffe and the steps stay exactly as they were prior to doing this, the horse is in perfect balance and control.

The same horse looking more balanced, with the neck longer.

CHAPTER 7

PASSAGE

The passage is a slow and elevated trot with a pronounced rhythm and cadence. The diagonal steps are raised during the forward movement to the same height as in the piaffe, but with a far longer moment of suspension. This extra elevation must be developed from a supple back and a lowering of the croup, with the joints in the hind legs bending to a greater degree as they take increased weight and propel the horse upwards and forwards.

Aids for Passage

The preparation for passage is as important as the actual aid for the movement, which is to close the legs to signify to the horse to elevate the trot steps. This is even more important than for other transitions, as the horse must be set up in the right speed with the correct amount of impulsion so that he is able to depart into passage without difficulty. I move the lower legs to a position slightly further back than when asking for piaffe and squeeze both legs at the same time in order to keep the horse straight.

Only a rider who has developed a balanced and co-ordinated seat is able to ask for passage, as the inexperienced rider will find it difficult to allow the passage to happen, even if they have been told what to do. The seat has an important influence on creating the bigger, more cadenced step. When the rider can sit deep and brace or relax the back muscles at will, he is able to encourage the upwards movement within the horse's natural impulsion. The hands must also allow the horse to come off the ground without inhibiting his desire to do so by being too strong.

The preparation for passage will vary, depending on the

A classical passage.

movement that is carried out before the passage is asked for. From piaffe, where the steps are similar and the horse does not have to be restrained from excessive forward movement, a slight indication with the legs whilst allowing the horse forward with the seat and reins is sufficient. However, when coming back from extended trot to passage, the steps must be shortened and the balance corrected. From rein back, a very clear and positive aid is recommended and the horse must be helped with the straightness and influenced forward with the seat and back.

Teaching Passage

The work leading up to teaching the horse to take the first passage steps varies according to the natural athletic ability and quality of movement with which each individual horse is blessed. All the requirements that are necessary to prepare for piaffe, and the piaffe itself, should be established before asking for the first steps of passage. The first steps can be asked for from collected walk, piaffe or from collected trot: I favour asking from collected trot as it is easier to have the horse in front of the leg, balanced and with more impulsion than from walk or piaffe.

The first objective is to create impulsion, for instance by riding a vigorous working trot. Next, this impulsion must be controlled and contained by riding transitions and half-halts. By restraining the horse at a slower speed, whilst maintaining energy, he is being encouraged to experiment and as a result will give a higher, slower step. If such a step is offered, the seat and hand allows it to happen; some horses produce the desired result immediately, while others can take weeks or months to get the idea. Some horses will actually quicken the rhythm instead of slowing it when they are first ridden in this way. If this happens, the process must be repeated patiently; in some cases the horse may require more impulsion and in others less. Then gradually improve the amount of contact until different reactions are produced.

Once some elevation is achieved it is vital to allow this lifting from the ground, because if it is restricted in the initial stages the horse may not try to do it again for a long time. It is therefore important that he is rewarded immediately and allowed to walk and relax before preparing and asking for a second time. The horse should not be asked for this extra lift to the stride until such time as the hind legs are well engaged underneath the body, the forehand is lightened, the outline rounded and possibly even made a little deep, and the horse is absolutely straight. If he is throwing his hindquarters out or putting too much weight on one or other shoulder, the steps will be unlevel from the start and the passage will not be balanced and through.

Difficulties and Corrections

Once the horse has become established in taking unlevel steps in the passage it is a very difficult problem to cure, and time is well spent creating the best possible preparation so that this

does not happen. It is advisable not to make too many steps of passage at a time, nor to practise it too often, until the horse's muscles and back are strong enough to cope with a longer duration of work. If the horse is asked to do too much too soon the neck, and especially the back, will suffer from stiffness and tension and the outline, quality of the steps and overall majestic impressiveness of the movement will be lost.

When the back becomes stiff and tired the horse will save himself by making passage steps with the front legs only, lifting the knees high with the shoulders flat and the hind legs dragging along the surface of the arena, unable to produce any elevated steps. This signifies incorrect training or a horse with a weakness, and it is a sorry sight. It is with this in mind that I like to perform all the passage work in training with the horse working in an extra-deep outline, to ensure that the back muscles are used correctly and are free from constriction and stiffness. The work should not be continued until the horse feels tired, and always try to finish on a good note.

Some horses can be extremely slow to realize that an elevated trot step is required. In such cases, working over cavaletti poles can help to produce the required result. The normal length of step of the collected trot must be established over five to seven poles on the ground. Thereafter, alternate ends of each pole can be raised on suitable blocks and the distance of each step shortened. As the horse reaches the first pole the rider should encourage an elevated step in a slower rhythm. This is achieved by taking the horse more securely with the leg whilst maintaining a correct deep seat and restraining the horse to a slower rhythm with the rein. Any attempt on the horse's part to step higher over the poles should be rewarded immediately.

The influence of an experienced trainer on the ground, standing beside the horse with a long whip, can also help to obtain the first few steps of passage. The horse will be more likely to accept this method if he has been worked in hand for piaffe. The stick should not be used in a way that causes tension and should only be applied in conjunction with the rider's own aids, and when the speed and rhythm are suitable to make the elevated steps. Some horses will only quicken their steps when the whip is in evidence, which defeats the object of the exercise and renders this method of achieving any elevation totally ineffective.

Horses will often make higher steps of their own accord when trotting through shallow water. This could be whilst riding on the beach at the edge of the sea or along a shallow,

OPPOSITE: *In this passage the hind legs are not sufficiently underneath the horse to take enough weight.*

Passage over trotting poles, to encourage more bending of the joints.

hard-bottomed river. These facilities are available to very few dressage riders; however, if the horse does not respond to the normal training aids in the school, the aids for passage can be given as the horse trots through shallow water, which may result in him understanding what is wanted.

Another method of teaching passage is to move forward from a well-established piaffe whilst at the same time maintaining the elevated steps. The horse must first learn to move forward with a smooth transition from piaffe into trot without hollowing. After this the rider can apply the passage aids as the horse takes the first trot steps forwards, and by containing the forward activity a little he will encourage an upward movement within the trot step. A person on the ground can help by touching the horse on the hind leg just above the hock to encourage the more elevated step as the horse goes forward. This must be done carefully, so that a snatching action does not develop in the passage in the hind steps. The same problem can occur with the forelegs if the stick is used on them.

Excessive use of the stick as an aid for piaffe and passage is usually made obvious to the onlooker by sharp, tense steps and a lack of body movement which detract from the overall picture – which should be of an athletic, floating movement with the horse working through the rein in an effortless manner. However, a horse can be idle and therefore lack any thoughts of springing from the ground, in which case the stick can support the rider's leg aid if used in the same area or on top of the haunches. Once the horse realizes what is wanted, the rider must make him obedient to his demands without any outside assistance.

Transitions

Once the horse has acquired the ability to make the passage steps, they should be further developed and established by making transitions from the collected walk and trot, before attempting to make any piaffe and passage transitions. These call for a great deal of balance and contained energy, and if they are started before the horse is fluent at the easier transitions from walk and trot both into and out of piaffe and passage, unwanted problems may arise that will spoil the smooth sequence of the piaffe–passage tour required for the Grand Prix and Grand Prix Special tests.

I prefer to ask first for the transition from piaffe into trot, and when the horse understands what is wanted I ask for passage, before attempting the transition directly into the slower speed and shorter steps of passage. This seems to keep the horse thinking forward and in front of the leg.

Bringing a powerful and very active horse back into piaffe can cause a certain amount of tension to start with, as some horses feel over restrained and will have a tendency to try to bound on. The ability to come back from collected trot into the 'half-collected' short steps (used as a preparation for the piaffe) will be most beneficial to the perfection of these difficult transitions.

The transition from collected walk into piaffe should be smooth and without any resistance. Once this is fluent, a transition from a slow, short trot which has less impulsion can be made into piaffe, and if the horse can manage this the trot can gradually be made more collected, more forward and more active. A perfect half-halt should be established before giving the piaffe aids. It helps if the rider gives the aids in the piaffe rhythm, so that the horse can pick up the piaffe without feeling pressurized or hurried. It is unwise to ask for piaffe if the half-halt has not had a good enough effect on rebalancing the horse, because if there is resistance in the mouth, or the steps have not been made short enough, the horse will not be able to make a good piaffe and it would be

ABOVE: *A perfectly balanced piaffe from which a transition into passage should be smooth and fluent.*

OPPOSITE: *This horse is working well through the rein and showing an impressive round outline.*

better to ride forward and try again. When piaffe is asked for from walk, the walk must slow down but retain an active hind leg in order to ensure a bouncy piaffe step and not just a higher lift of the hind leg while the corresponding diagonal foreleg is still on the ground.

Until the horse can make the transition from collected trot into piaffe the transition from passage into piaffe should not be attempted. It is very important at this stage of the training that each step up the ladder is very carefully established, and perfected, before attempting the next one up. So many problems can develop through hurrying these difficult transitions and making the horse tense and worried, possibly establishing bad habits that are then very difficult to eradicate.

All the transitions into and out of piaffe must therefore

become progressively more difficult and should not be asked for from more than a few piaffe steps at first. The more piaffe steps that are asked for the more disturbed the horse's balance will be and the more tension will be generated in the mind, so a lot of tact and feel must be applied initially. The actual transition can become fluent in quite a short space of time, once the horse understands what is wanted and can handle the required amount of impulsion to do it. In fact, when this stage is reached the transition from passage into piaffe is usually more fluent, although initially more difficult for the horse to comply with, than the transition out of piaffe, in which the horse is inclined to lurch out of piaffe on to his forehand, leaving the hind legs behind. Tremendous strength, suppleness and muscle control is needed on the horse's part to perform this movement to perfection, while the rider must be very careful to allow the horse to work forward and through the hand in alll these transitions, otherwise unlevel steps and hollowing can occur.

Allowing the horse to work forward and through the hand is the most important criterion for obtaining perfection in all these transitions. It is not easy to restrain the horse from moving forward too much whilst keeping him thinking forward, and at the same time allowing the energy created by the rider to be channelled through the body correctly in an upwards direction.

Aids During the Transitions

The horse must first of all be very familiar with the aids for each movement, and the change of leg aid must be made in a way that does not upset the flow of either movement. Horses vary in their reaction to different aids. If the aid is given too hastily, the horse may jump forward or leave out the last steps of piaffe. As these are counted and accuracy is at a premium, the rider must be aware of this. If the aid is given too slowly or too late, steps of walk may occur between the transitions, or too many piaffe steps may be shown.

When first finding the best way to manage these transitions the rider must learn to feel how the horse reacts, and the slight progressive movement forward that the horse makes should not be reprimanded but gradually reduced, until all the transitions are fluent enough for the Grand Prix test. It goes without saying that a rider should not attempt piaffe and passage transitions until such time as his leg aids are under perfect control and do not make any uncontrolled movement that could confuse the horse. All the movement through the horse's body during this work should be accepted by the rider's own body and hands in a supple manner, while the legs must remain in close contact and very still unless actually asking for a change in the work.

The Bridle

It is desirable that the horse is taught the piaffe and passage in a snaffle bridle to ensure that he works correctly through his back and into the hand. If the horse becomes tense and rejects the restraining aids for forward movement while he is still learning to elevate, he may drop the bit and come behind the bridle. Control during transitions is then impossible and this can be quite a difficult fault to overcome. It is better to get the horse working through his back and into the snaffle rein correctly and then move on to a double bridle, with possibly a more refined control, once the horse is on the aids in all transitions.

The Outline

I prefer to have the horse in a very deep outline when first making the transitions so that he will learn to come up with the shoulders correctly. Ultimately, the head and neck should be proudly raised from the shoulders, which are also elevated. In this outline you will obtain maximum brilliance from the steps. If the horse is allowed to use the muscles on the underside of the neck to raise the forehand, he will not use his shoulders to the greatest advantage.

If the horse can maintain piaffe steps in a round outline while the rider gives and retakes the rein, then he is well on the way to becoming strong enough in his muscles and sufficiently balanced to produce very good transitions when asked.

'Passagey Trot'

If during the development of the collected trot the horse shows a degree of elevation, usually with a stiff back and straight hind legs, this is not to be confused with passage. It is called a 'passagey trot' or 'swimming trot' and as the suspension is not linked with the qualities already mentioned for passage it is not acceptable.

If this occurs, the horse should be ridden actively forward in a more normal rhythm. This problem is often caused by the rider asking for too much impulsion in the collected trot before the horse is supple or round enough, which results in the rein is usually being too strong – a lighter contact may

remedy the problem. This trot may also be used as an evasion to working round and using the back correctly. Whatever the cause, this false rhythm is not usually maintained throughout the collected trot work as it disappears while the horse is making lateral steps, and this eventually manifests itself in the horse showing trot work in several different rhythms, which cannot be condoned.

Once the passage is well established it will add cadence to the collected trot, without the trot becoming 'passagey'. The two must always be clearly defined to the onlooker. The horse must not be allowed to become too complacent about the passage steps – laziness will reduce the energy necessary to produce the best possible results. This can happen if the passage is practised too often or for too long. The trot half-pass steps can be improved if followed by riding a length of passage and then back to half-pass. By doing this the horse will learn to maintain an improved suspension during the forward and sideways movement, but it is important that the half-pass is not ridden in half-passage or half-collection, but in a more enhanced and active collected trot.

The transition from extended trot into passage requires that the horse has the ability to come back from the maximum forward movement and then contain the impulsion and channel it into the more elevated steps. At first the passage after the extension is usually too free, and several half-halts have to be ridden to slow it down. It is advisable to go from extension into a few steps of passage and then let the horse walk until such time as he can passage for longer without becoming strong in the rein or leaving the hind legs too far out behind him. Both eventualities can occur if the extended trot preceding the transition has not been in perfect self-carriage. If you try to perform this movement before the horse is ready, you can cause an unnecessary deterioration in the quality of the passage.

The opposite is the case when piaffe or passage is per-formed from rein back. The horse is then well balanced with weight transferred on to the haunches, so he should find it much easier to go directly into either movement. As with all transitions, it is important to keep the horse straight. The downward transition from extended trot, and whilst riding the rein back, are two very vulnerable movements for main-taining straightness, and the rider must be able to keep total control of the horse's shoulders by applying the shoulder-in aids when necessary to a greater or lesser degree.

OPPOSITE: *A rounded outline allowing maximum use of the back.*

145

The Tests

The first test in which the piaffe and passage transitions are asked for is the Intermediare II. In this test you have to ride one departure into piaffe from passage, and one from collected walk, plus passage from collected trot and then from the piaffe. Initially these movements are shown on the track, as it is an easier place to ask the horse; at Grand Prix level they are required in the centre of the arena. There is no continuous sequence of transitions at Intermediare level, as is required at Grand Prix level. At this level you have to show every possible transition, including transitions into passage from extended trot, rein back and collected walk, as well as frequent changes from piaffe to passage to piaffe, and from passage into canter. This is obviously far more difficult than the Intermediare II level test and I feel it is a mistake to try to ride a horse through the Grand Prix test in competitions until such time as these transitions can be executed very fluently at home, and even away from home but not in a competition.

Horses have to be very physically fit to perform Grand Prix level work. If a horse has been laid up or has been given a holiday, it is a mistake to start the very collected movements, and especially the piaffe and passage, too soon or before the muscles and general condition warrant it.

A young horse will take years to develop into a strong and powerful Grand Prix horse, although some talented and very trainable horses may well be able to do the movements at an earlier stage than others. Reaching Grand Prix level with a horse that is eight or nine years old is soon enough. It can be done earlier, but often horses that are pushed too early show signs of strain or have difficulty with one movement or another and will often not stay sound as long as those that have been given time to mature and strengthen. The ability to show collection in all gaits must not be hampered by tension or weakness.

A horse that is trained to Grand Prix level will often then take a further three years to perfect the work and show the whole test to his utmost ability. After this, the horse that is awarded high marks will be capable of qualifying for the Grand Prix Special and all the years of dedication, hard work and patience will have been worthwhile.

CHAPTER 8

FREESTYLE
TO MUSIC

The introduction of dressage to music has given the sport an entirely new image with the general public. This is because it is something that the dressage enthusiast can relate to, as well as providing a more easily recognizable artistic aspect to a sport which at times can give the uninitiated the impression that it is merely a continual drudge round in circles, until finally reaching the dizzy heights of Advanced level with its top hat and tail coat.

It is possible to make a Freestyle to Music test at all levels from Novice up to Grand Prix. The requirements at each level are set out on test sheets, leaving the competitor free to make a programme which contains the necessary movements in the time allowed, and ride them to music of their own choice. The test should take into account the make and shape of both horse and rider, and the degree of training that has been attained, and be designed to add charisma and interest to the paces and movement.

Below Advanced Medium it is difficult to produce a very interesting programme, as the level is clearly set and a higher standard of work must not be shown. However, the lower tests will give valuable practice to the rider in sorting out some suitable music, learning to ride to it, getting the transitions correct as the music changes and not at a chosen place in the arena, and so on. By the time this has been done in Novice, Elementary and Medium classes, the rider should be sufficiently experienced to produce a really good Freestyle at the more advanced levels. The more difficult the movements that are ridden to music, the more impact is made on the spectators. Tempi flying changes, piaffe and passage are particularly impressive, especially if the rhythm and beat of the horse are well co-ordinated with the music.

As far as the programme at any level is concerned, it is better to show movements that the horse can do easily and well, which enable you to keep the quality of the paces a priority, rather than try to show a difficult pattern before the horse can cope with it. This will only spoil the paces and overall picture. It is especially important to work out a progamme which will enable you to keep the horse in a steady rhythm that fits the beat of the music, because if a strong beat is chosen it can be very obvious if the horse gets out of tempo. If the music acts as more of a background the rider will get away with a slight change of rhythm, particularly in movements such as the half-pass or extended trot.

It is a mistake to use a programme that makes it difficult for the judges to mark the movements in either direction. It is much easier to judge a test that is balanced and has a 'mirror image' pattern on either rein. This will make the judges happier, particularly if they are not concerned as to whether they have seen all the set requirements of the test. It is not easy to judge an Advanced Freestyle to Music class, so there is no point in making their task even more difficult.

Making a good Freestyle programme and choosing suitable music is not something that can be done in a hurry. You should allow several weeks before the final rehearsal prior to the day of the competition. It is vital that the music and the programme are very familiar, so that you do not have the added strain of remembering where to go or when the music will change from trot to canter or vice versa.

There are two options open to a Freestyle competitor: one is to contact a professional who specializes in making tapes for competition purposes, and the other is to make a tape at home with help from friends. If you choose the first option, this person will come and watch the horse working, measure the beat of walk, trot and canter on a metronome, and bring samples of music to establish the rider's taste. They will discuss the duration of walk, trot and canter music required, and put a rough idea of the programme on to a video tape for reference. A pattern that suits the music can then be perfected by the rider at leisure. The recorded music must finish 15 seconds before the maximum time allowed in order to compensate for the different speeds that can occur on a variety of equipment used at competitions. The Novice tests are of a shorter duration than those at Advanced level.

If you choose the option of making the tape at home or with the help of a friend, you will have to have access to the necessary equipment to copy and edit the chosen pieces of

OPPOSITE: *Extravagant steps and a good position in half-pass that would look magnificent when ridden to music.*

This powerful horse is well engaged whilst turning within his own length on the circles of the pirouette. He would earn good marks in a Grand Prix Freestyle to Music.

music. This is not an easy task and can take hours. It is certainly not a job that should be undertaken the day before a competition!

I personally make a programme that contains the set movements and shows the degree of difficulty that I feel the horse can cope with in relation to the standard of training he has achieved. I put the test on a video tape and then, while watching the horse work on video, try various pieces of music to decide which tracks best suit the movements – it is vital to match the rhythm of the horse's strides in each pace to the music. When the music has been chosen the pattern can then be changed to suit the various expressions. For example, the extended trot may look better on a stronger beat during the trot music, or the tempi changes fit a certain passage in the music used for canter. This can be sorted out once a tape of the correct length has been produced. Ideally, you should try to have the end of the programme finishing simultaneously with the natural ending of the music.

Any music may be used, but it must not distract the judges – they may be offended by some singing tracks or way-out, noisy pop numbers with unusual instruments. However, there is always the risk that the judges may not appreciate classical music, so on the whole it is best to choose light, tuneful music that fits the horse's paces and enhances his way of going. To add sophistication to the Freestyle performance, it is better to have the walk, trot and canter in the same key, and I also like to use the same instruments, or a mixture of instruments, with one being dominant in all three pieces. The canter is the most difficult to match to music because of the three beats and then a moment of suspension. It usually works out that the canter beat is almost the same as the music suitable for the passage, although the rhythm of both of these can vary with each horse. A horse with a big, active collected canter will be at a much slower rhythm than a horse with shorter, less springy steps.

The height of luxury is to persuade a band, orchestra or smaller group of musicians to produce tailor-made music especially for the horse. This can be extremely expensive, but the end result is usually most impressive and way above that which the amateur can produce on tape.

The horse's way of going must be correct and the result of the classical training, with the correct rhythm in all movements. It would be wrong, for example, to make pirouettes to a very slow beat just for effect, when keeping the correct rhythm and footfalls is what is required in pure dressage tests

– dressage should not be turned into a type of ballroom dancing show. The classical training and beliefs that have evolved from the early days of the ancient Greeks and Zenophon should not now be misused for the sake of creating a spectacle. The horse's gaits, which have been developed through correct training, along with the sophisticated and harmonious control with which the rider can show the required movements with complete excellence, will produce a truly stylish and breathtaking performance.

A Grand Prix horse showing impressive cadence and a clearly defined moment of suspension in trot. These steps look most impressive performed to music.

CONCLUSION

The previous chapters have been directed towards the training of the competition horse from Novice standard through to Grand Prix, with the underlying assumption that the competition horse should also be classically trained. But what do we mean by classical dressage? Are there forms of classical dressage that are not suitable for competition?

There are two ways of defining 'classical': one is simply to say that it is training based on accepted, long-standing tradition; the other definition is a little more meaningful, and states that it should incorporate measures of simplicity, harmony, proportion and excellence in the same way as 'classical' music or art.

If dressage is an art, then this poses a whole new set of questions. It must be termed a living art, that has progressively created and produced work now accepted as being traditional, with its roots based on the teachings of the old masters. One can ask, 'Is the work performed by the traditional riding masters to be revered'? Many pictures portray them with unacceptably sharp spurs and monstrous curb bits that are no longer used. Therefore, are the professionals of today better or worse than the old masters? Unfortunately, there is no way of comparing them. Many textbooks have been written over the years, but it is impossible to be certain if the authors could practise what they preached, as most of them were riding before the days of video and film. However, the films available of dressage over the years since filming has been possible are not very impressive when one compares the top riders of two or three generations ago with the medal winners of today.

If the above is true and we think of classical dressage as following the traditional method, then whose method should

we follow? One hopes that all that is best in the training of the horse to the highest degree will become even more refined and orthodox, and the short cuts and discrepancies will be eliminated, so that the horse will never be abused or degraded whilst fulfilling a rider's ambition to get to the top in competition.

OPPOSITE: *This horse is lowering his croup and remaining well on the bit in a classical piaffe.*

155

A beautiful, classically correct passage.

For centuries riders have been attempting to convert half a ton of raw, ignorant power into a willing, obedient and elegant athlete. There is little debate about the finished product: a horse that is supple, obedient, balanced and powerful, and yet happy to perform what is asked of him. This can only be achieved by the best and most civilized methods that have been passed down from generation to generation. It is only at such time when the worst has been discarded that the training can truly be said to be classical, and if it is to be considered as a form of art, then it is worth remembering the quote of a wise dressage master: 'Art ends where violence begins.'

A good height of step and a confident passage across the centre of the arena, demonstrating competition dressage as an art form.

INDEX

Page numbers in *italic* refer to the illustrations

Advanced level tests 27–31
Advanced Medium level 26
aids:
  'between the inside leg and the
    outside rein' 40–1
  counter change of hand 70
  flying changes 73–6, *74–5*, 77, 86–7
  giving away reins 40–1
  half-pass 63, 64
  horse in front of leg 41–2, *42–3*
  passage 130, 133–4, 138–9, 142–5
  piaffe 116–17, 118–20, 126, 129, 130
  pirouette 94–5, 96, 97, 104
  shoulder-in 50
  straightening the horse 49
  tempi changes 90
  travers 55
arenas, size 23

back:
  bending *36*, 37, *37*, 47–9, *49*
  passage 133, 137, *144*
  piaffe 130–2
  rounding *38*
  straightness 18–20
balance:
  development 32–3
  flying changes 83
  piaffe 125
bending *36*, 37, *37*
  lateral work 46–9, 60
'between the inside leg and the outside
  rein' 40–1, 47
bit:
  contact and accepting 14–16, *17*
  passage and piaffe 143
bridles, passage and piaffe 143

cadence 13
  Freestyle to Music *153*

Cadre Noir, Saumur 120
canter:
  collected 44
  counter canter *74–5*, 76, 81, 98, *98*,
    106, *106*
  counter change of hand 34, 64, *64–7*,
    68, 70
  'disunited' canter 12, 71, 72
  flying changes 26, 71–90, *73*, *78–85*
  Freestyle to Music 152
  half-pass in 26, 61–3, *62*, *63*
  lateral work 61–4
  pirouettes 12, 32, 51, 55, 92–4,
    97–100, *98–100*
  rhythm 11–13, *12–13*
  shoulder-in 51
  suspension 12, 71, 72
cavaletti poles, practising passage 137,
  138
cavesson, piaffe work in hand 118, 119,
  119
circles:
  'between the inside leg and the
    outside rein' 40–1
  shoulder-in 51
classical dressage 154–6
collection 18, 44
  canter 44
  counter change of hand 68
  piaffe 112
  suppleness 34
  trot *42*, 44, 110, 112, 135
  walk 44, 110
contact with the bit 14–16
counter canter *74–5*, 76, 81, 98, *98*, 106,
  106
counter change of hand 34, 51, 64–70,
  64–7
crookedness 13, 19, 47, 49
croup:
  passage 133
  piaffe 113, 120, 122, 124, *129*, *131*,
    155

diagonal aids, piaffe 130
diagonal line, pirouettes on 106–7
'disunited' canter 12, 71, 72
double bridles, passage and piaffe 143
drawing back from the rein, flying
  changes 88

Elementary level competitions 21–2
equipment, work in hand *117*, 118
extended trot *19*, *25*, 145

Fédération Equestre International (FEI)
  tests 27, 28
feet, piaffe 112, *114*, *124*
films 154
  see also videos
flatness, canter 12–13
flexion 16, *16*, 37, *37*
  lateral work 45–6
flying changes 23, 26, 32, 34, 71–90,
  73, *78–85*
  aids 73–6, *74–5*
  changing 'late behind' 71, 87–8
  counter change of hand *65*, *66*, 68, 70
  drawing back from the rein 88
  Freestyle to Music 147
  riding a sequence 81–3, *84–5*
  running away from the leg 86–7
  swinging hindquarters 86
  teaching 76–81
  tempi changes 88–90, *89*, *91*
forehand, turn about 45
forelegs, piaffe 123–4, *125*, 126, *128*
Freestyle to Music 147–53, *148–51*
  choosing music, 149–52
  choosing programme 147–9
  pirouettes 93, 94
  sequence changes 90
front legs:
  extended paces 24, *25*
  flying changes 71
  passage 137
  piaffe 123–6, *125*, *126*, *128*
  pirouettes 92

shoulder-in 49
straightness 18–20
travers 54

gaits:
Advanced Medium level 26
collection 44
extended 24, 26
rhythm 9–13, *10–13*
transitions 26, 44
see also canter; trot; walk
Grand Prix 29, 30, *30*
Freestyle to Music *153*
passage 146
pirouettes 108–10
Grand Prix special 31

hacking, practising piaffe 127–8
'half-collected' trot 139
preparation for piaffe 116
half-halt:
transition to passage 145
transition to piaffe 139
half-pasade 98
half-pass 27, *34*, 55, *56–9*
in canter 26, 61–3, *62*, *63*, 98–9, *99*
counter change of hand 34, 64, 68,
69, 70
faults 63–4
Freestyle to Music *148*
impulsion 41–2
lateral work 45, 46, 47
in trot 26
half-pirouette 93, 100–1, *107*, *110*
halt 19
in hand work, piaffe 117–20, *117*, *119*
head, flexion 46
'head to the wall' 60
headcollar ropes 118
hind legs:
collection 18
extended paces 24, *25*
flying changes 71
impulsion 18
passage 133, 135, *136*, 137
piaffe 126, *128*
pirouettes 92
shoulder-in 49
straightness 18–20
travers 54
hindquarters:
development of muscles 32, *32*, *33*
engagement 45
flying changes 86
passage 135
piaffe 112, 122, 128, *129*
pirouette 96
preparation for pirouette 99, 102
straightening the horse 49

impulsion 14, 16, 17–18, *19*
counter change of hand 69
half-pass 41–2
lateral work 45

passage 133, 135
piaffe 113, 120
shoulder-in 54
in hand work, piaffe 117–20, *117*, *119*
Intermediare I 28
Intermediare II 28–30, 146

'jogging' 116
judges, Freestyle to Music 149, 152

knees:
passage 137
piaffe 119, 124, *126*

'late behind', flying changes 71, 87–8
'late in front', flying changes 71
lateral work 24–6, 45–70
in canter 61–4, *62*
counter change of hand 64–70, *64–7*
exercises 45–6
flexion and bend 46–9
half-pass 55, *56–9*
renvers 60
shoulder-in 48, 49–54, *52–3*
travers 54–5, *54*, *55*
in trot 60
lead ropes 118
leg aids:
'between the inside leg and the
outside rein' 40–1
counter change of hand 70
flying changes 73–6, *74–5*, 77, 86–7
half-pass 64
horse in front of leg 41–2, *42–3*
passage 133–4, 139, 142–3
piaffe 116–17, 120, 129, 130
pirouette 94–5, 96, 104
shoulder-in 50
straightening the horse 49
tempi changes 90
travers 55
leg yielding 45, 63, *63*
legs:
extended paces 24, *25*
flying changes 71
impulsion 18
passage 133, 135, 137
piaffe 123–6, *125*, *126*, *128*
pirouettes 92
shoulder-in 49
straightness 18–20
travers 54
see also hindquarters
long reins, piaffe work in hand 121–3,
121–3
loosening up 34–7, *35*
lungeing 34

Medium level competitions 22–3, 24
mirrors 101
muscles:
development 32–3, *32–3*, 100
relaxation 14, *15*
stiff side 18–20
music *see* Freestyle to Music

neck:
bending 37, *37*, 46–7
development of muscles 32
flexion 46
loosening up 35–7
passage 137
piaffe 130–1, *131*, *132*
straightness 18
transitions to passage 143
Novice level competitions 21

Olympic Games 31
'on the bit' 16, *17*
one-time changes *see* tempi changes
outline:
Advanced horses *41*
Medium level competitions 22, 24
Novice horses *40*
passage 137, *141*
piaffe 130–2, *130–2*
transitions to passage 143, *144*

paces *see* gaits
pacing 10
pasade 55, 82, 98, *98*, 100
passage 29, 133–46, *134–44*, *156–7*
aids 130, 133–4, 142–3
difficulties and corrections 135–9,
136, *138*
Freestyle to Music 147, 152
from rein back 145
half-pass in 61
piaffe or passage first? 112–13
teaching 135
tests 146
transitions 19, 133, 134, 138, 139–46,
140–1, *144*
'passagey trot' 143–5
piaffe 112–32, *113–32*, 155
aids 116–17
difficulties and corrections 123–9
Freestyle to Music 147
from rein back 145
leg aids 130
outline 130–2, *130–2*
piaffe or passage first? 112–13
pirouettes from 93
preparation for 115–16, *115*
transition to passage 19, 134, 138,
139–42, *140*
work in hand 117–23, *117*, *119*, *121*
work in long reins 121–3, *121–3*
pillars, piaffe between 120
pirouettes 92–111, *93–111*
advantages and aims 92–4
aids 94–5
canter 12, 32, 51, 55, 92–4, 97–100,
98–100
Freestyle to Music *150–1*, 152
Grand Prix 108–10
half-pirouette 93, 100–1, *107*, *110*
practising 100–6
preparation and build-up
exercises 96, *96*

Prix St George 106–8
  in walk 51, 92–4, *94*, 110–11
poles, practising passage 137, *138*
Prix St George 28, 106–8

quarter-pirouette 96

rein aids:
  counter change of hand 70
  drawing back from 88
  flying changes 86, 87
  giving away 40–1
  half-passes 63
  passage 143–5
  pirouette 94–5, 97
  shoulder-in 50
  tempi changes 90
  travers 55
rein back 19
  piaffe or passage performed from 145
reins:
  long 121–3, *121–3*
  piaffe work in hand 119
  side 118, *119*
relaxation 14, *15*, 34
renvers 45, 46, 60, 61, *61*
  preparation for pirouette 99–100, *100*
rhythm 9–13, *10–13*
  Freestyle to Music 147, 149
rider:
  flying changes 76–7, 86
  Medium level competitions 26
  horse in front of the leg 41–2, *42–3*
  see also aids
rising trot 21
rounding *38*

Schaukel 28
seaside, practising passage 137–8
seat:
  flying changes 76, 86
  passage 133, 134
'self-carriage' 14, 16, 21
serpentine loops 73, 106, *107*
'shoulder-fore' position 50
  flying changes *82*, 83
shoulder-in 22, 27, 37, *52–3*
  aids 50

'between the inside leg and the
  outside rein' 40
  into renvers 60, *61*
  into travers 60, *60*
  lateral work 45, 46, *47*, *48*, 49–54
  straightening the horse 20
shoulders:
  flying changes 86
  transitions to passage 143
side reins 118, *119*
sitting trot 21
slopes, practising piaffe 128, *129*
snaffle bridles, passage and piaffe 143
Spanish Riding School, Vienna 106,
  106, 120
spurs, piaffe 117, 129
sticks:
  flying changes 77
  piaffe 116, 117, 129
  piaffe work in hand 118, 119–20, 126
  practising passage 137, 138–9
straightness 18–20, *20*
submission 16–17, *18*
suppleness 14, *15*, 34–7, *36*, 45
suspension:
  Freestyle to Music *153*
  passage 145
'swimming trot' 143
swinging hindquarters, flying
  changes 86

'tail to the wall' 60
tapes, Freestyle to Music 149–52
temperament, and piaffe 129
tempi changes 32, 81, 88–90, *89*, *91*
  Freestyle to Music 147, 152
tempo 13
Thoroughbreds:
  flying changes 77
  piaffe 120, 122, 123, *125*
transitions 26, 44
  Freestyle to Music 147
  to passage 19, 133, 134, 138, 139–46,
    140–1, *144*
  to piaffe 139–40
travers 45, 46, 54–5, *54*, *55*, 60, *60*, 61
  preparation for pirouette 99–100, *101*
trot:

collected *42*, 44, 110, 112, 135
counter change of hand 64–7, 69
Elementary level 22
extended *19*, *25*, 145
Freestyle to Music 152, *153*
'half-collected' 139
half-passes 26
lateral work 60
Novice level 21
passage 133, 135
'passagey' 143–5
piaffe 112, 115–16
rhythm 10–11
rising 21
shoulder-in 51–4, *53*
sitting 21
transition to passage 139
transition to piaffe 139, 140
travers 54
working trot *30–1*
trotting poles, practising passage 137,
  138
turn about the forehand 45

videos 13, 101, 149, 152
voice aids, piaffe 116, 117, 118
voltes 98, *98*, 102

walk:
  collected 44, 110
  free walk 44
  Freestyle to Music 152
  pirouettes 51, 92–4, *94*, 110–11
  rhythm 9–10, *10–11*
  transition to passage 139
  transition to piaffe 139–40
Warmbloods:
  flying changes 77
  piaffe 122
water, practising passage 137–8
whips *see* sticks
'working through' 14
working trot *30–1*

zig-zag on the centre line 46, 51, 63,
  64–9, *64–7*